Bible Curriculum
STUDENT'S BOOK

A curriculum that teaches moral objectives from the Bible.

These arts and crafts are simple enough for most children to do with little help from adults. Wide grey lines around the pictures help children know where to cut. Dotted lines are for folding. Included are the art and crafts pages, some of the games and a verse for each Bible lesson.

Have fun crafting and exploring God's Word!

This book is to be used together with the Teacher's Guide.

Copyright 2016 iCharacter Limited. All rights reserved.

Old Testament Stories

Story 1: God Makes the World (Creation) ....4 *Diligence*
Story 2: The First Sin (Adam and Eve) ....6 *Self-control*
Story 3: Following God (Noah's Ark) ....8 *Obedience*
Story 4: The Tall Tower (Babel) ....10 *Humility*
Story 5: Abraham Relies on God ....12 *Dependance on God*
Story 6: Waiting for a Baby (Abraham and Sarah) ....21 *Patience*
Story 7: A Wife for Isaac (Rebekah) ....22 *Initiative*
Story 8: Jacob Cheats (Jacob and Esau) ....25 *Honesty*
Story 9: A Special Dream (Jacob) ....28 *Encouragement*
Story 10: A Colorful Coat (Joseph) ....29 *Comparing*
Story 11: A Helpful Sister (Myriam) ....30 *Responsibility*
Story 12: Crossing the Sea (Moses) ....31 *Confidence*
Story 13: God's Ten Commandments (Moses) ....33 *Justice*
Story 14: A Noisy Battle (Joshua) ....37 *Willingness*
Story 15: A Woman Goes to Battle (Deborah) ....38 *Service*
Story 16: A Crazy Idea (Gideon) ....37 *Flexibility*
Story 17: The Strongest Man Ever (Samson) ....39 *Decisions*
Story 18: Gathering Wheat (Ruth) ....41 *Faithfulness*
Story 19: Praises to God (Hannah) ....45 *Praise*
Story 20: Take Time to Listen (Samuel) ....47 *Attentiveness*
Story 21: A Shepherd Boy (David) ....48 *Caring*
Story 22: Facing a Giant (David and Goliath) ....68 *Courage*
Story 23: Songs to God (Kind David) ....70 *Devotion*
Story 24: A Very Wise King (Solomon) ....75 *Wisdom*
Story 25: A Temple for God (Solomon) ....76 *Worship*
Story 26: The Feeding Birds (Elijah) ....78 *Endurance*
Story 27: A Widow in Need (Elijah) ....78 *Unselfishness*
Story 28: Seven Baths (Naaman) ....80 *Determination*
Story 29: A Wee Little King (Joash) ....81 *Teamwork*
Story 30: Three Brave Men (Fiery Furnace) ....86 *Conviction*
Story 31: Surrounded by Lions (Daniel) ....87 *Peer-pressure*
Story 32: Rebuilding the Walls (Nehemiah) ....88 *Perseverance*
Story 33: Queenly Beauty (Esther) ....92 *Beauty*
Story 34: Into the Fish's Belly (Jonah) ....93 *Availability*

New Testament Stories

Story 35: The King is Born 94	*God's love*
Story 36: Kingly Gifts (Wisemen) 96	*Admiration*
Story 37: At the Temple....................................97	*God's word*
Story 38: Talk about Jesus (John the Baptist) 99	*Boldness*
Story 39: Jesus picks His Disciples 101	*Following Jesus*
Story 40: Hanging Out With Jesus 103	*Kindness*
Story 41: Water to Wine Miracle 106	*Cheerfulness*
Story 42: Jesus Calms the Storm 110	*Gentleness*
Story 43: Doctor Jesus (Little Girl Back to life) ...114,116	*Faith*
Story 44: Is That a Bird? (Blind Man Healed) 115	*Asking God*
Story 45: Lost and Found (Parable of Lost Sheep) 116	*Being responsive*
Story 46: Friends help out (The Paralyzed Man) 116	*Friendship*
Story 47: A Boy Shares his Lunch....................119	*Sharing*
Story 48: Stop and Listen (Mary and Martha) 120	*Jesus first*
Story 49: A Wounded Traveller (Good Samaritan) 122	*Compassion*
Story 50: The Party Boy (Prodigal Son) 124	*Forgiveness*
Story 51: A Thankful Return............................125	*Gratefulness*
Story 52: A Changed Man (Zacchaeus) 126	*Repentance*
Story 53: Into Jerusalem 128	*Enthusiasm*
Story 54: Not Just a Snack (Communion) 129	*Communion*
Story 55: Jesus on the Cross 131	*Salvation*
Story 56: He is Risen 133	*Easter*
Story 57: Jesus Goes to Heaven 136	*Hopefulness*
Story 58: Flames of Fire (Holy Spirit) 137	*Holy spirit*
Story 59: Good News to All 139	*Witnessing*
Story 60: Heaven to Come (John's Visions) 141	*Heaven*
Extra Bible verse cards..................................143	

Story
1

1

2

3

4

5

6

Story
1

a Bible verse on diligence:

Diligent hands that work hard, make you rich.

(Proverbs 10:4)

Story
2

I can close the door to temptation.

_____
(your name)

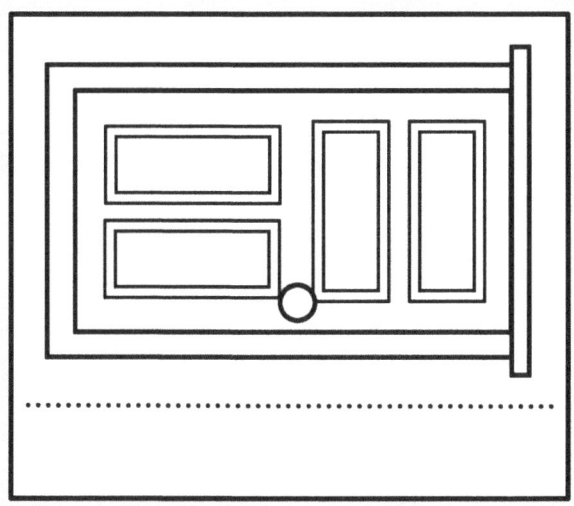

a Bible verse on self-control:

Above all things, guard your heart.

(Proverbs 4:23)

Story **2**

Story
3

Story **3**

 a Bible verse on obedience:

Do what is right and good in God's sight.

(Deuteronomy 6:18)

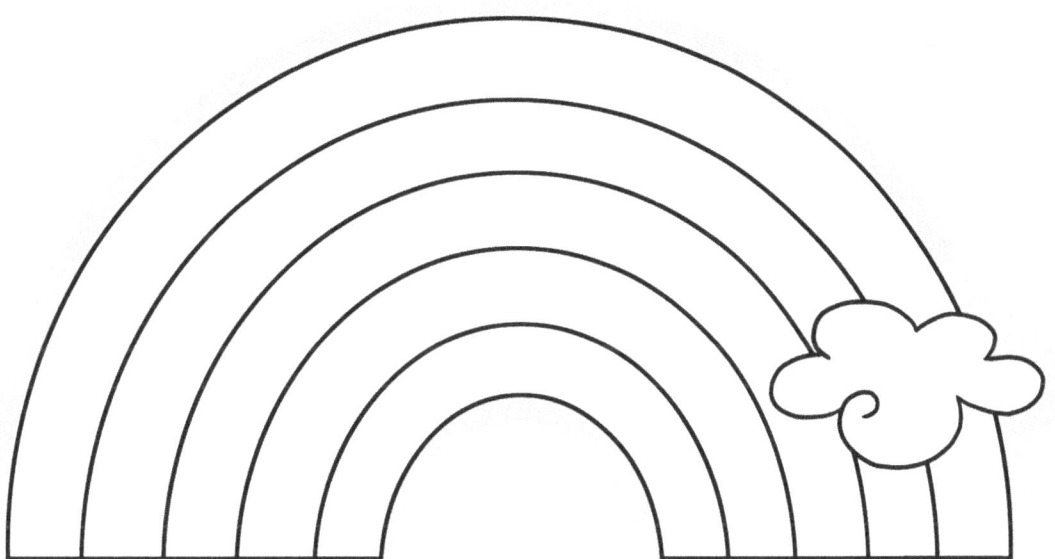

Story
4

a Bible verse on humility:

God goes against the proud, but gives grace to the humble.

(James 4:6)

Story
4

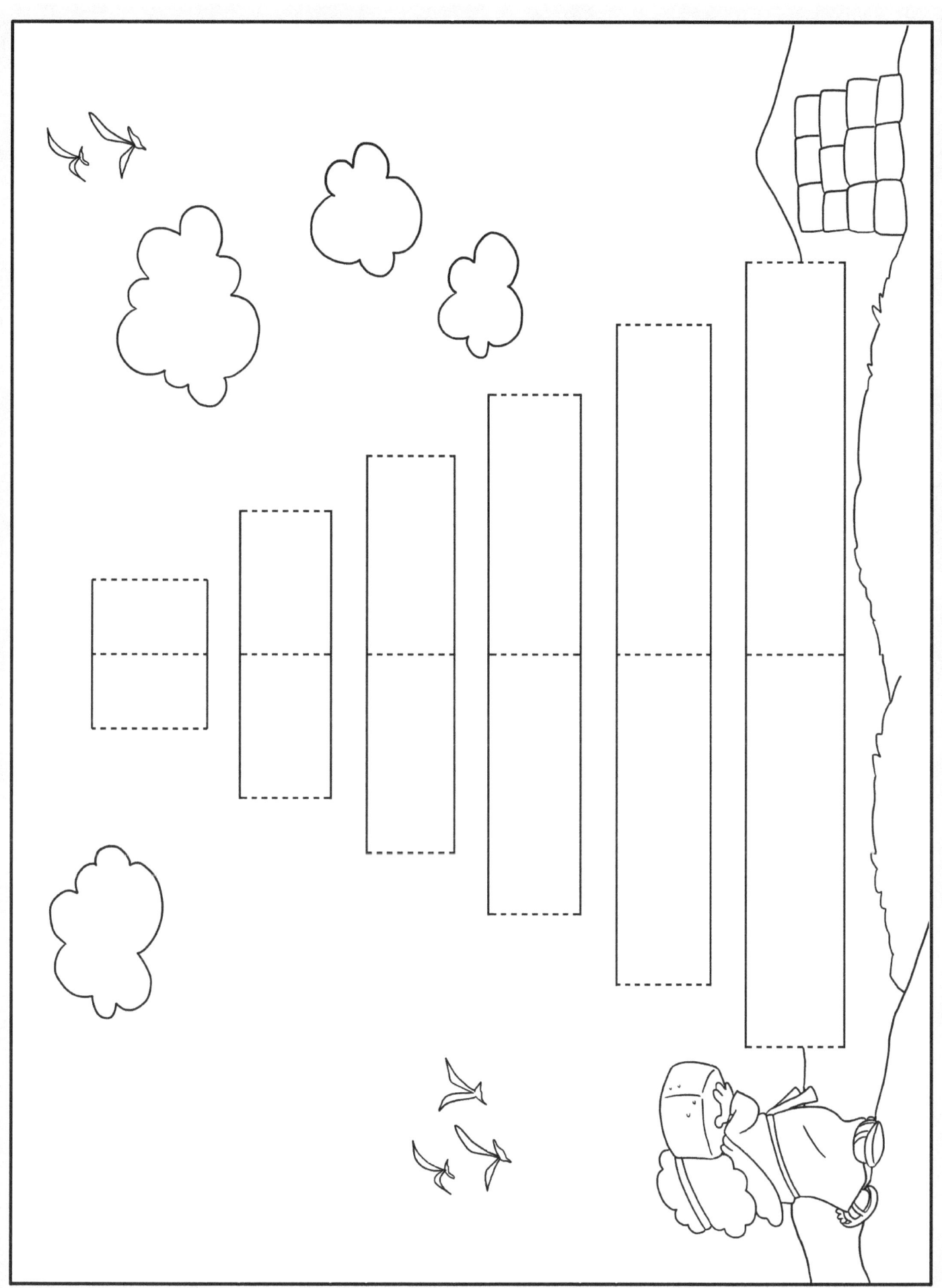

Story
5

a Bible verse on dependance:

Show me your ways, dear God, and teach me Your paths.

(Psalm 25:4)

Story
5

Story 5

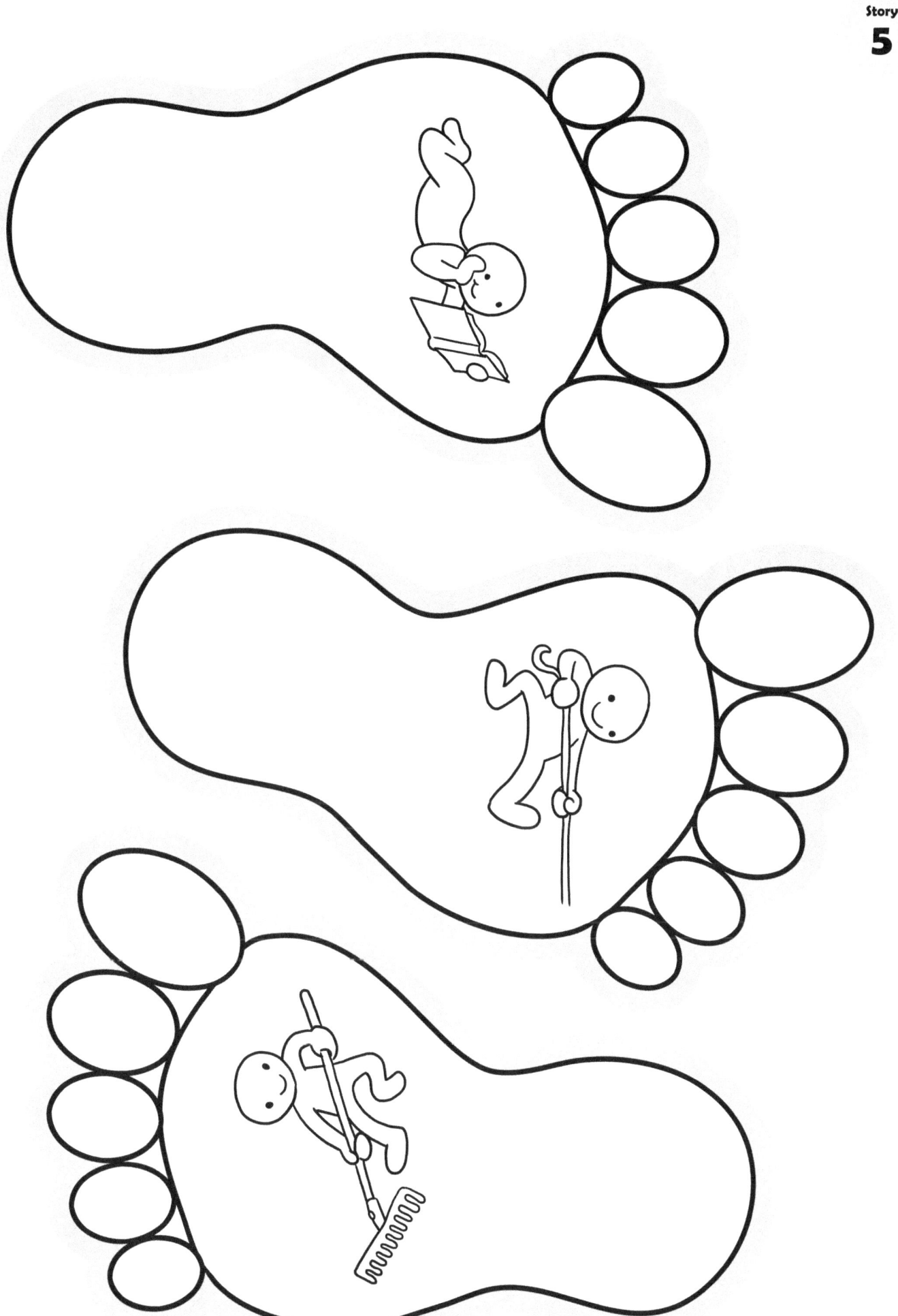

14

Story
5

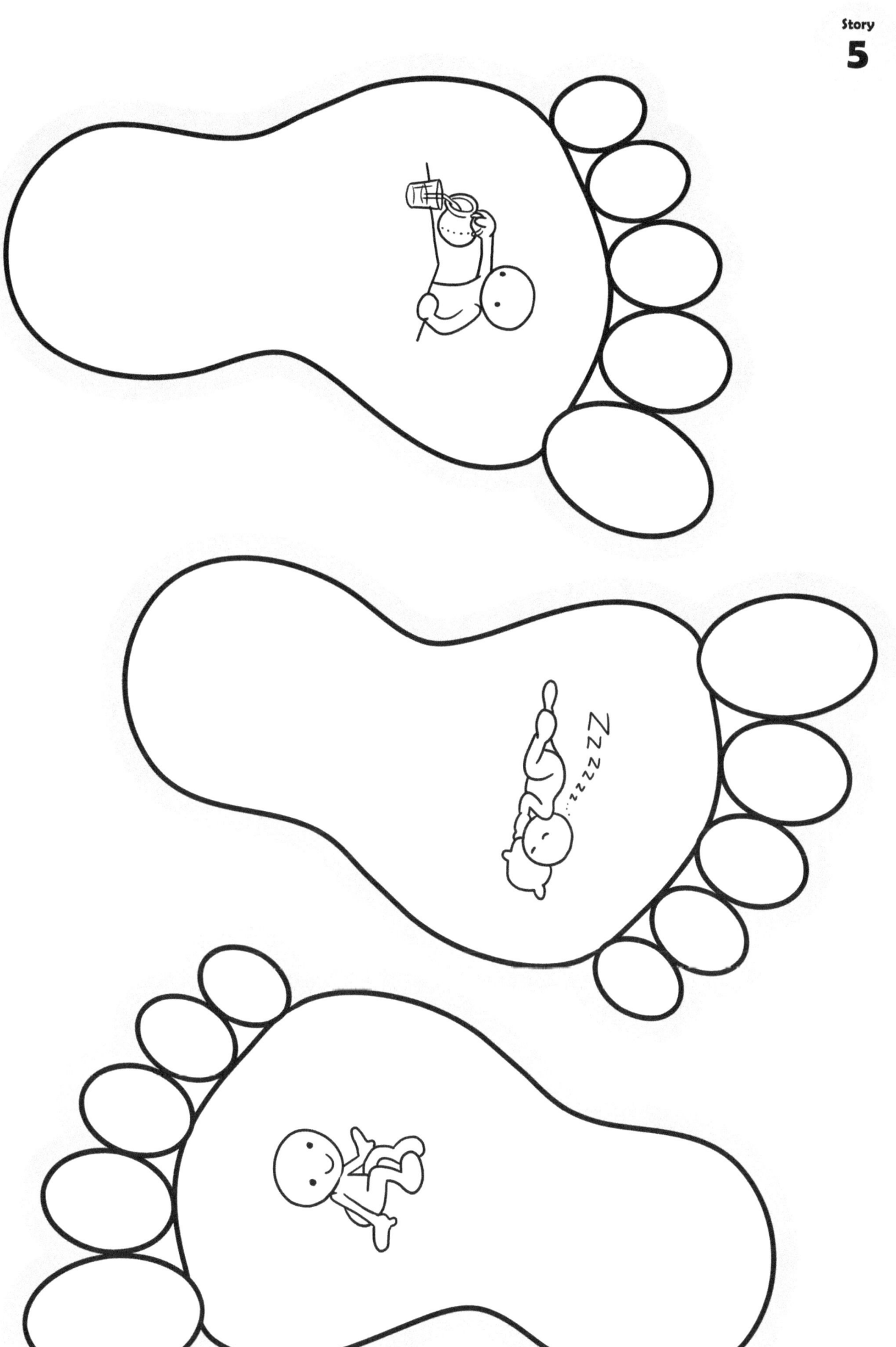

15

Story **5**

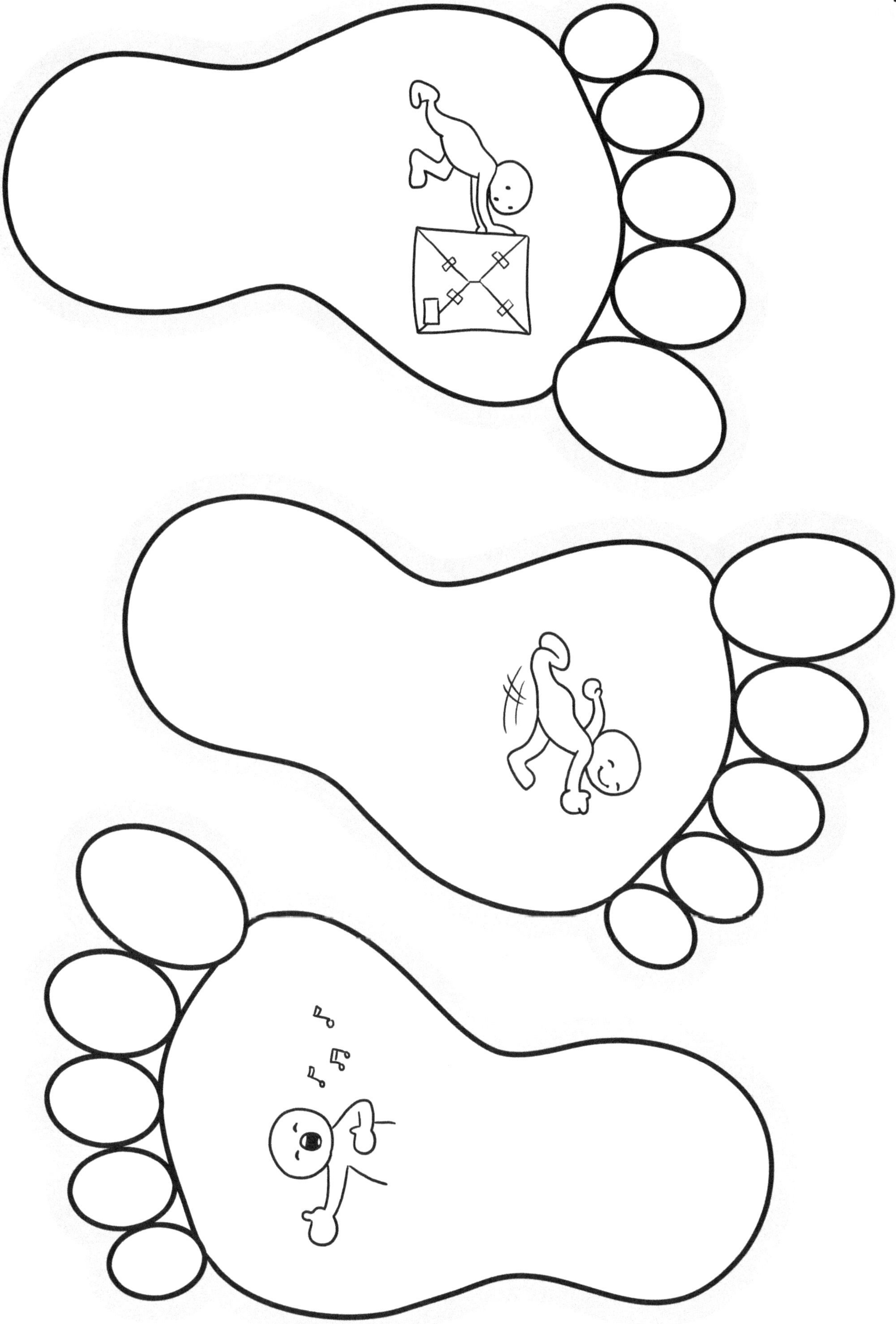

16

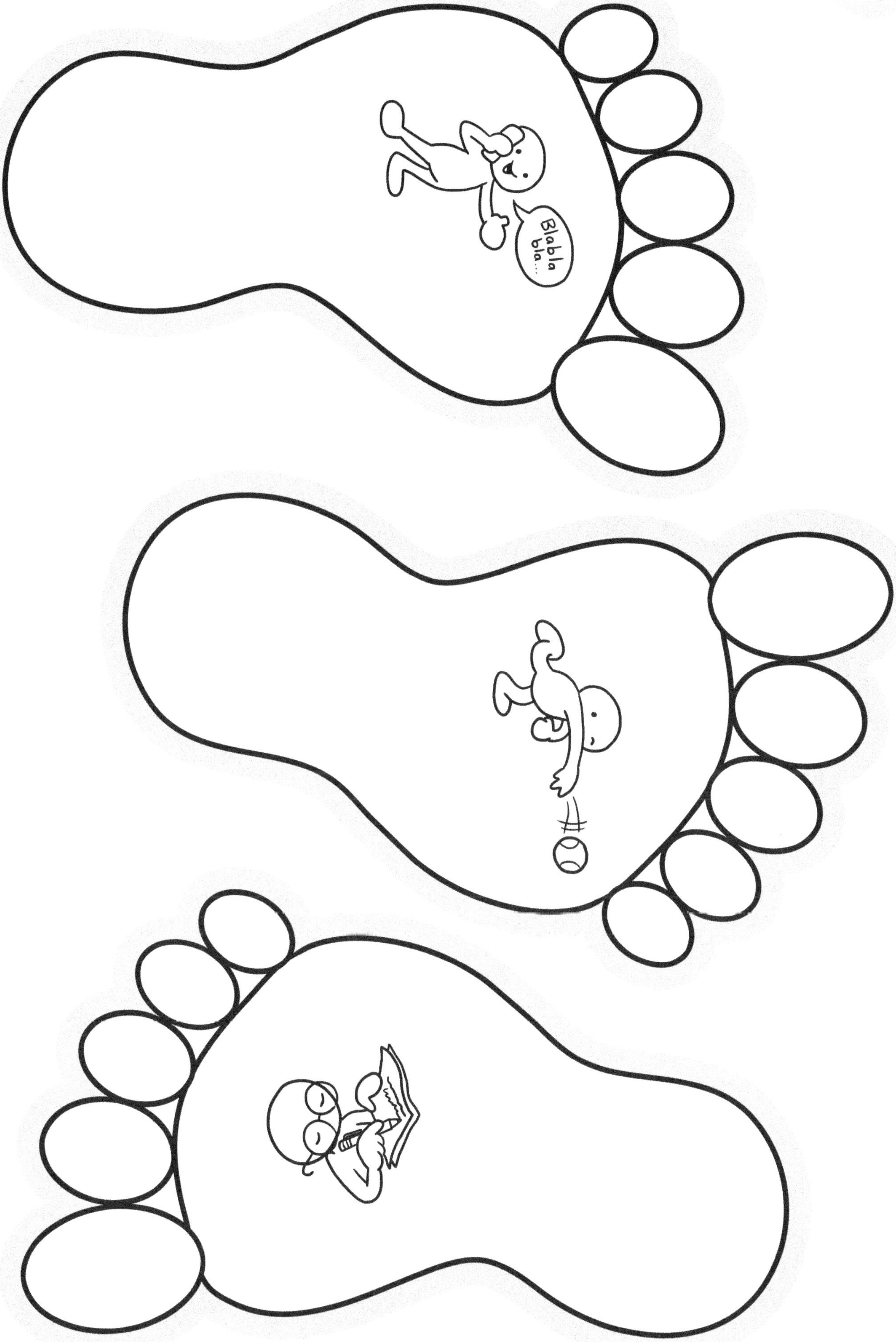

Story
5

Story
5

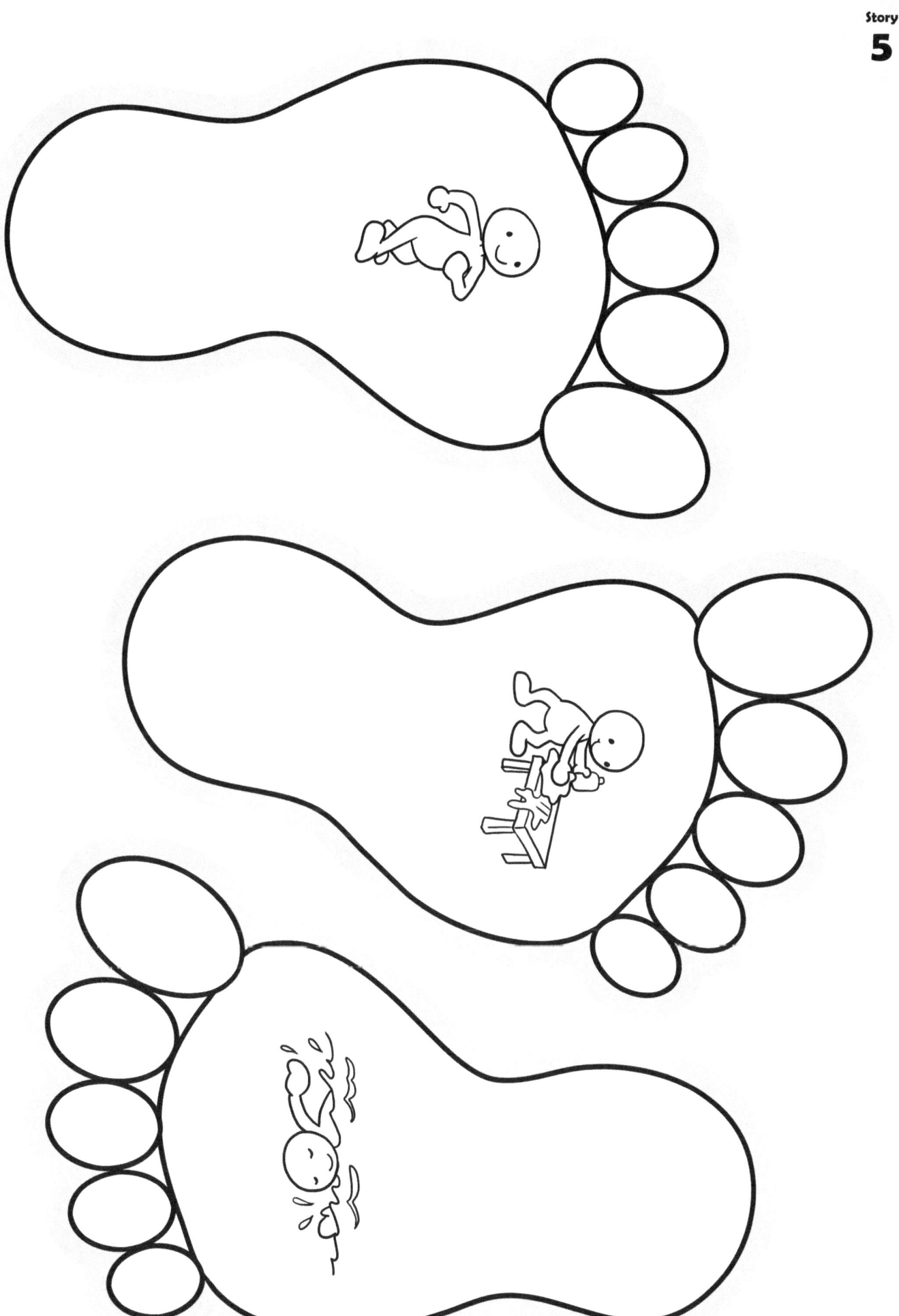

Story
5

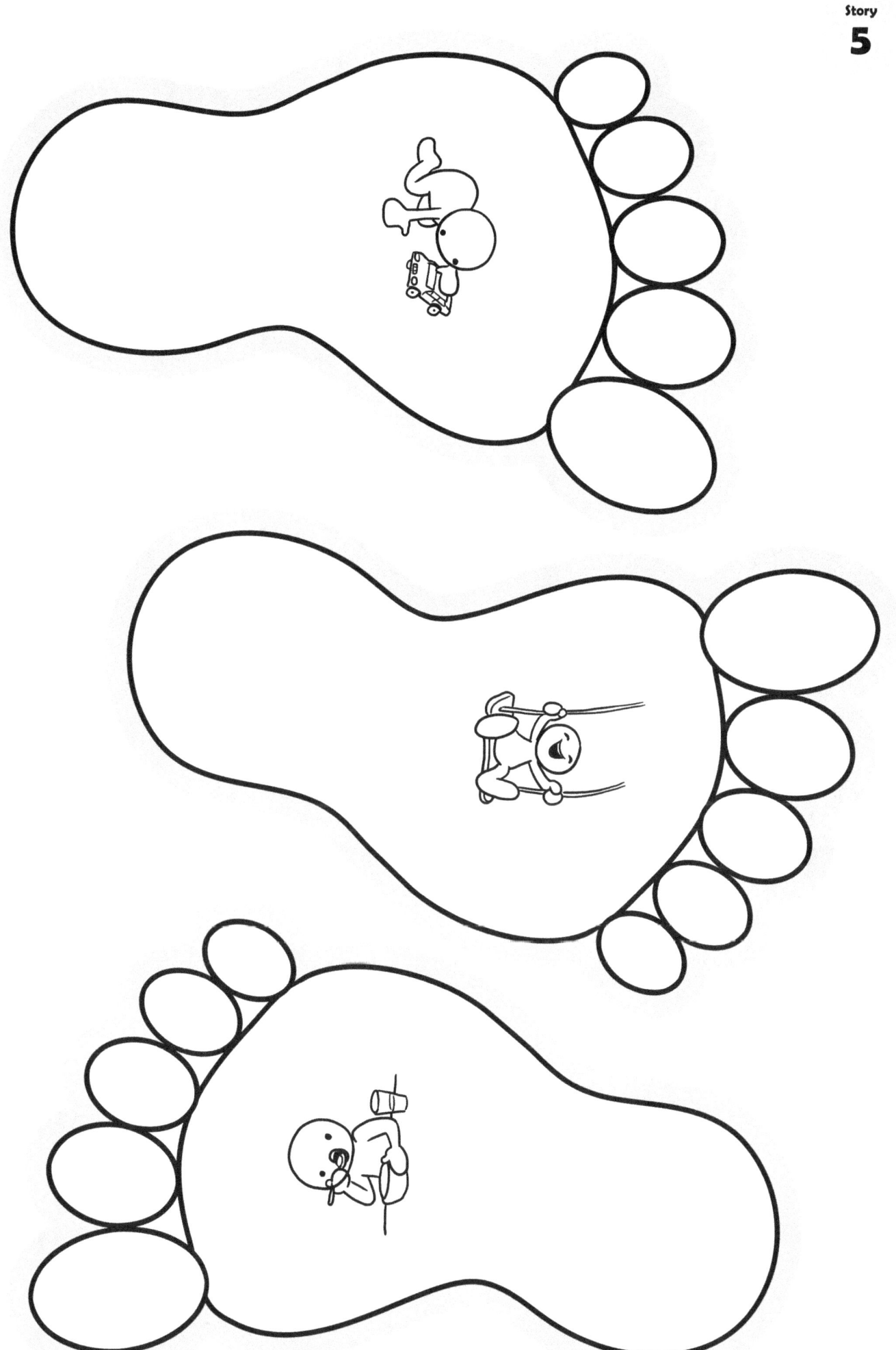

Story 5

Land

Water

Sky

Story **6**

Abraham and Sarah waited patiently for a baby.

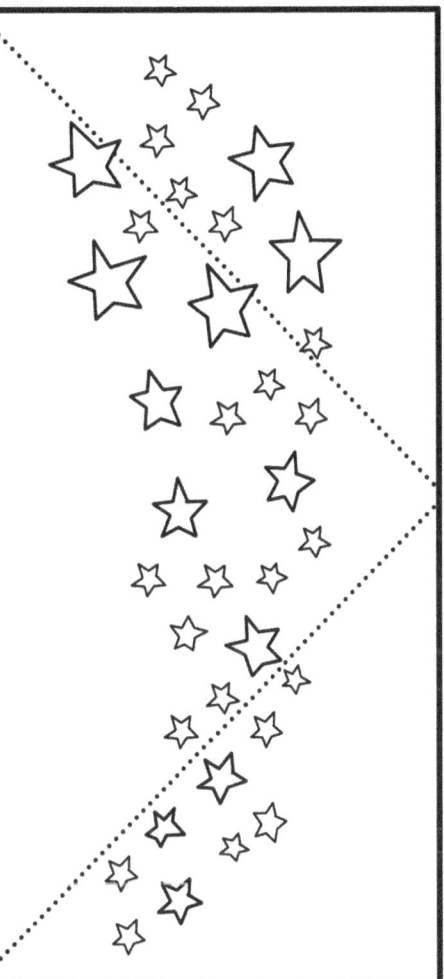

God blessed them with a cute baby boy named Isaac.

 a Bible verse on patience:

Wait for the Lord.
Be strong in heart and
be patient for Him.

(Psalm 27:14)

Story 7

a Bible verse on initiative:

Be generous and ready to share.

(1 Timothy 6:18)

Story
7

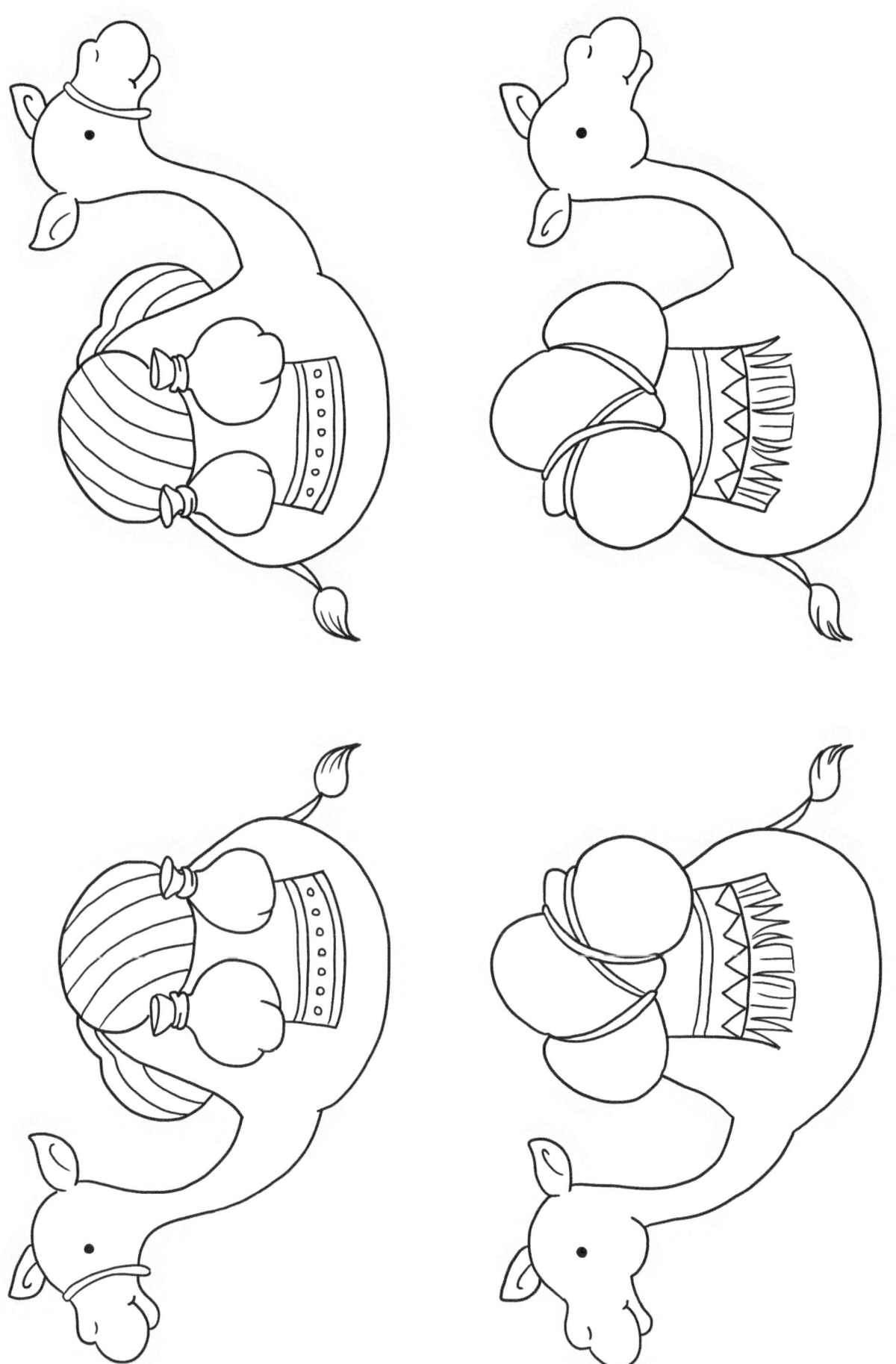

24

Story **8**

Story 8

Story
9

 **a Bible verse on encouragement:**

It is God who gives me courage and strength and makes my way perfect.

(Psalm 18:32)

Story
10

 a Bible verse on comparing:

Do your very best to live in peace with everyone.

(Hebrews 12:14a)

Story
11

Story
12

a Bible verse on confidence:

Nothing at all is impossible with God.

(Luke 1:37)

Story
11

↓

a Bible verse on responsibility:

He who is faithful in the little things will also be faithful with much.

(Luke 16:10)

Story 12

32

Story
13

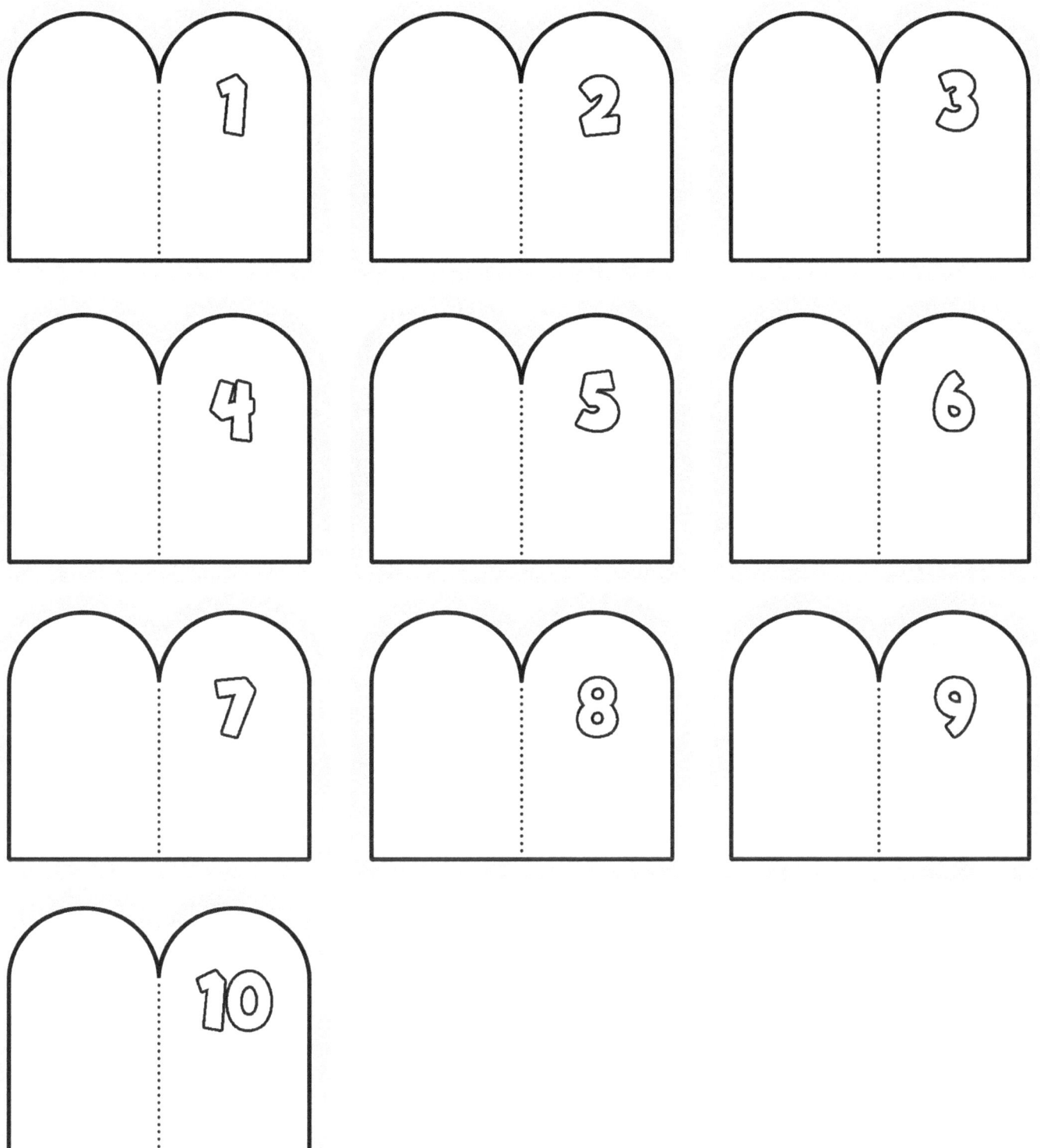

33

Ten Commandments

If you love Me, follow
My commandments.

(John 14:15)

Story 13

"Do not kill." (Exo. 20:13) We shouldn' do anything that would hurt others.

"Do not commit adultery." (Exo. 20:14) Husbands and wives should stay true to each other and love each other always.

"Do not steal." (Exo. 20:15) Taking things that do not belong to us is stealing; like taking candy from the store without paying for it. We shouldn't take anything that isn't ours.

"Do not be a false witness against your neighbor." (Exo. 20:16) One little lie can often grow into more and bigger lies. We should be honest and always tell the truth.

"Do not want what your neighbor owns." (Exo. 20:17) You should be happy for other people's blessings and not be sad or angry that you don't have the same things that they do.

"Do not put any other gods in place of Me." (Exo. 20:3) God should be number 1, above all. We should love and serve the Lord with all our heart, might, mind, and strength." (Deu. 6:5)

"Do not make any statues of gold to worship." (Exo. 20:4) Idolatry may take many forms. Some people do not bow before statues today, but instead they put other things before God like money, material possessions, or fame.

"Do not misuse the name of the Lord your God." (Exo. 20:7) We should keep our mouth clean by using the Lord's name respectfully and reverently just like brushing our teeth keeps our mouths clean.

"Remember the Sabbath day, to keep it holy." (Exo. 20:8) Take a day a week to rest and spend time with God.

"Honor your father and mother." (Exo. 20:12) We should love, obey and respect our parents.

Story **13**

1. Love God more than you love anything else.
2. Don't make anything in your life more important than God.
3. Say God's name with love and respect.
4. On the seventh day of the week, spend time with God.
5. Love and respect your dad and mom.
6. Never hurt anyone.
7. Be faithful to your husband or wife.
8. Don't take things that aren't yours.
9. Always tell the truth.
10. Be happy with what you have, instead of wanting what others have.

a Bible verse on justice:

If you love Me, follow My commandments.

(John 14:15)

Story
15

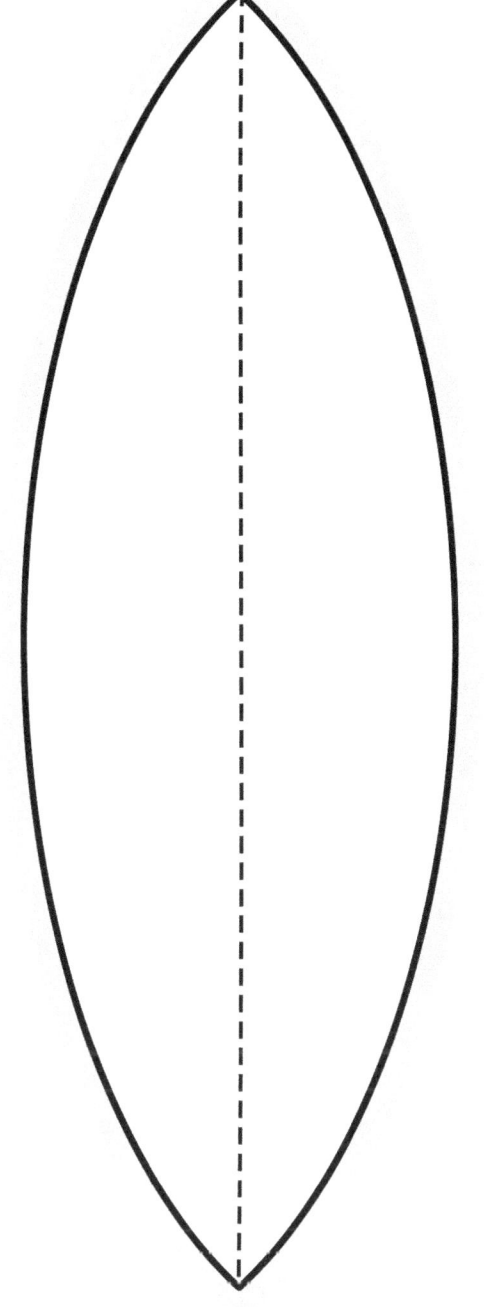

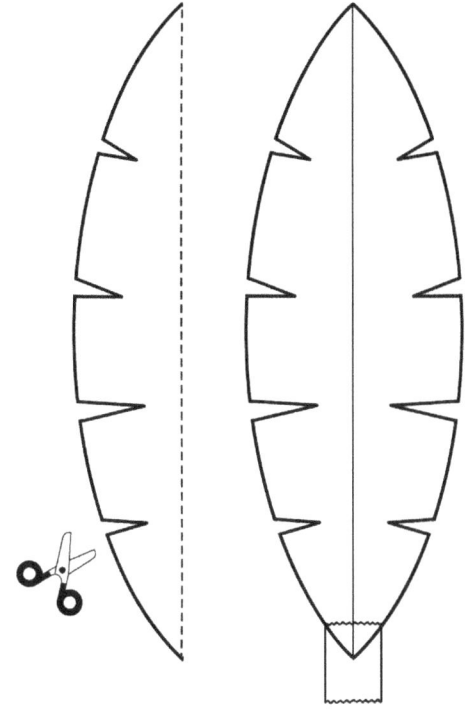

a Bible verse on service:

Work hard and cheerfully at whatever you do, as though you were working for the Lord.

(Colossians 3:23)

38

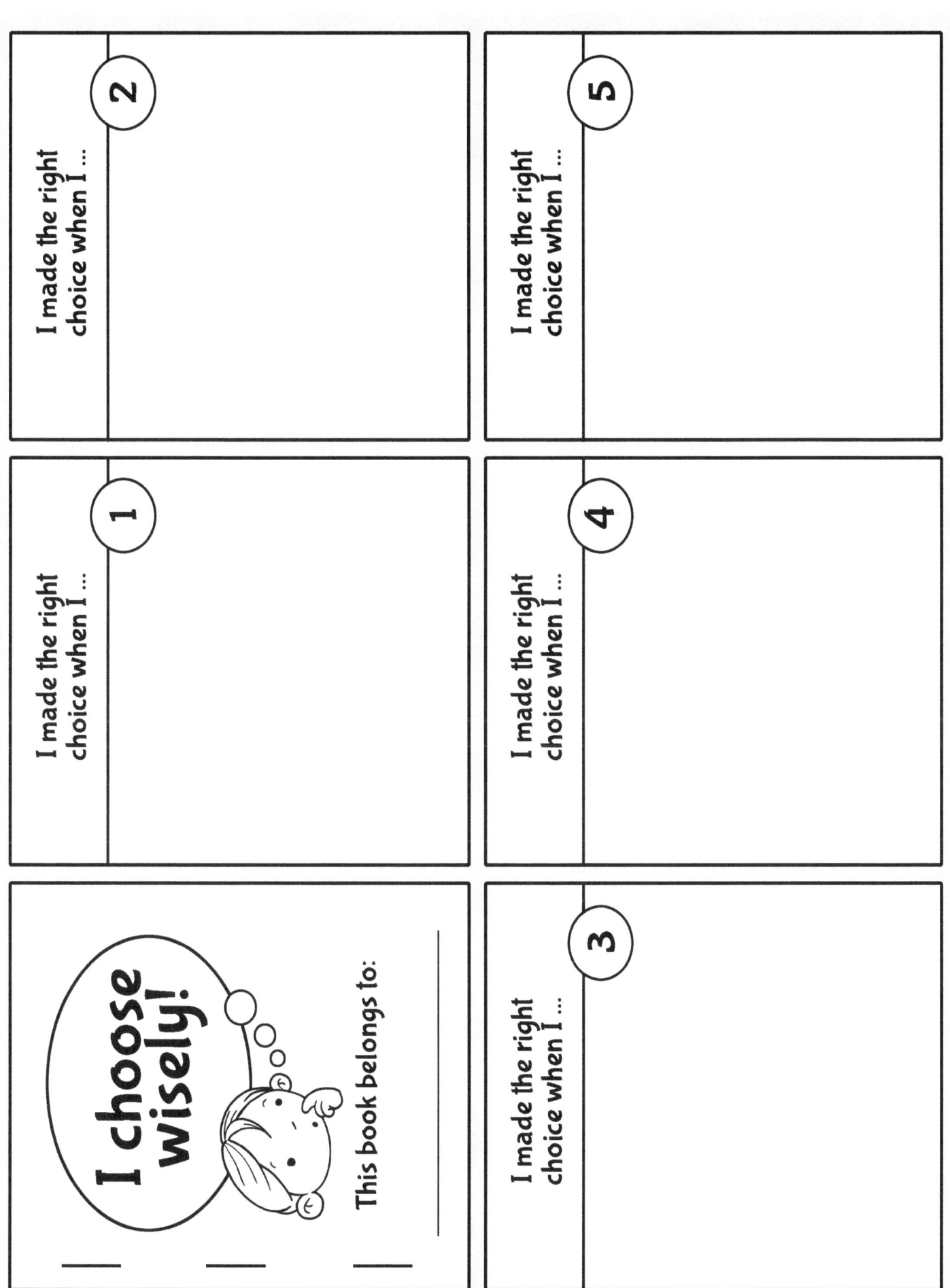

Story
18

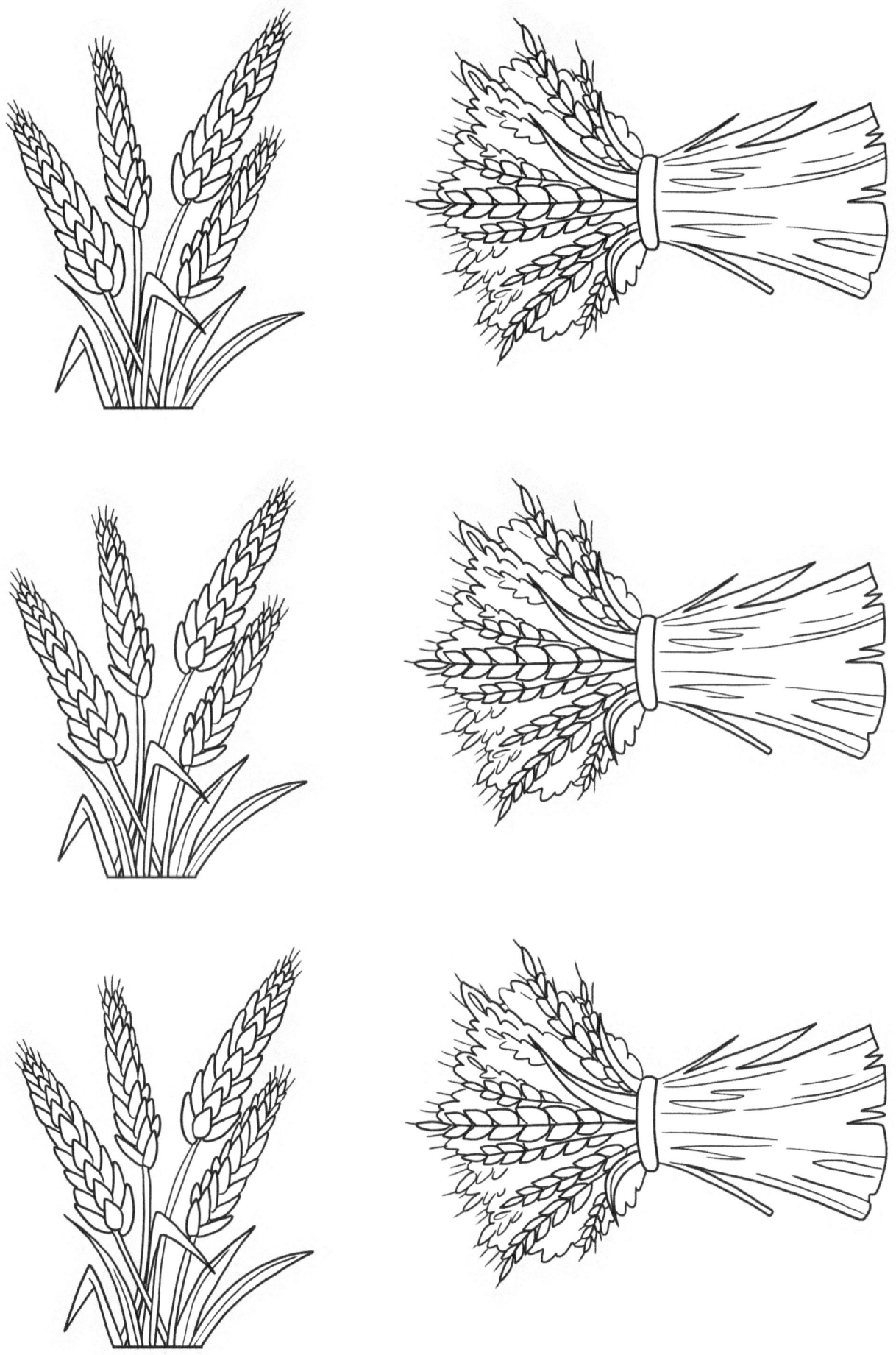

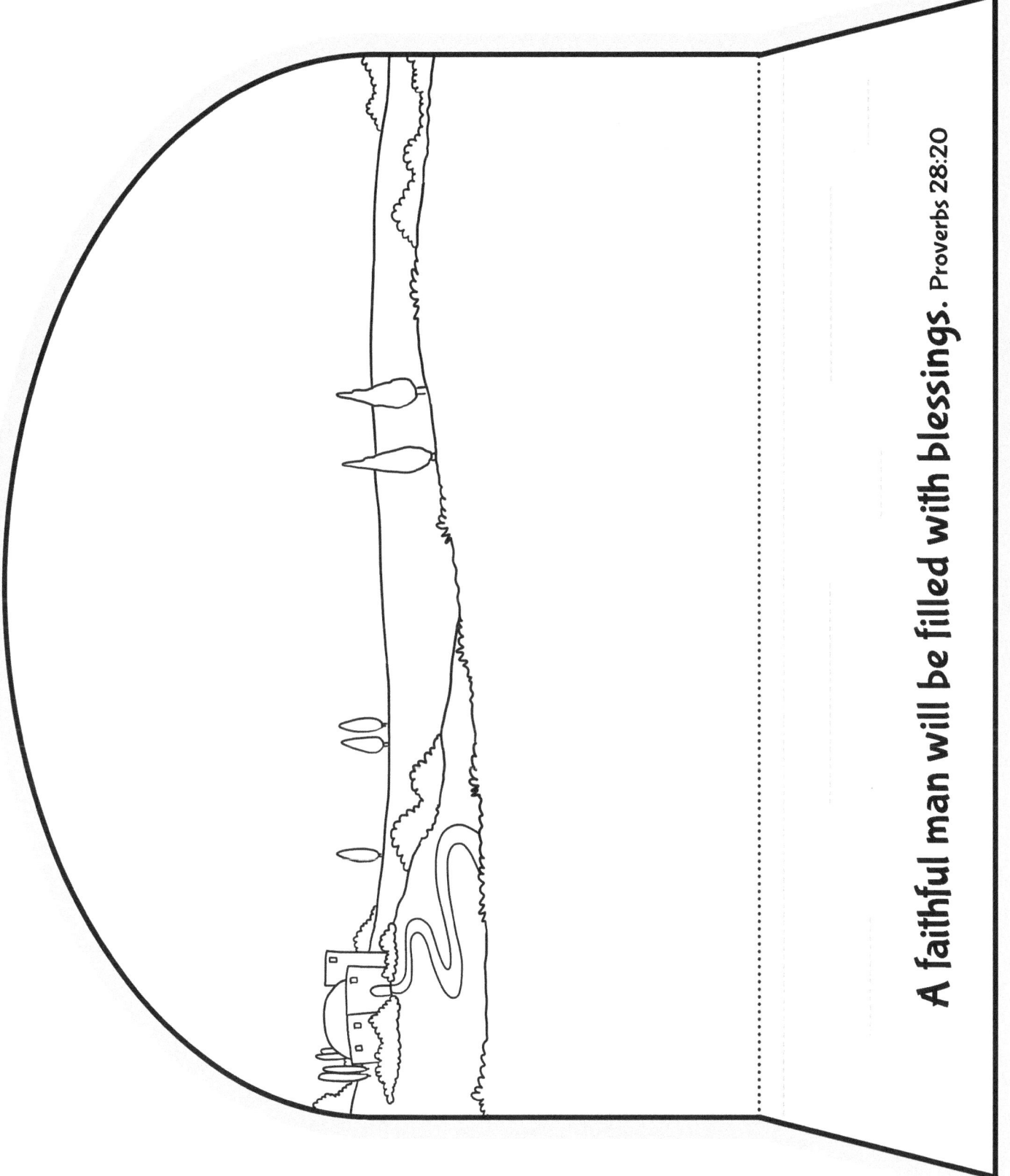

Story
18

43

Story
18

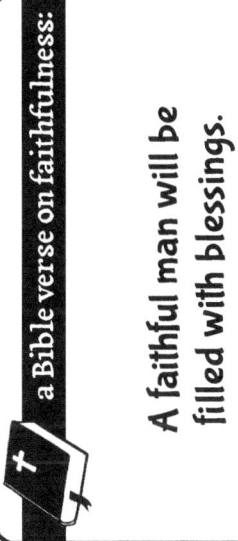

a Bible verse on faithfulness:

A faithful man will be filled with blessings.
(Proverbs 28:20)

44

Story
19

a Bible verse on praise:

Be glad and rejoice
for surely the Lord has
done great things.

(Joel 2:21b)

45

Story
19

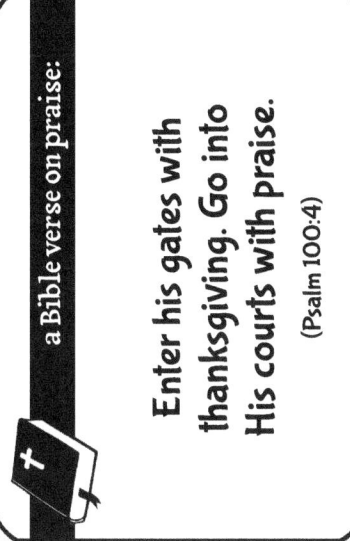

a Bible verse on praise:

Enter his gates with thanksgiving. Go into His courts with praise.

(Psalm 100:4)

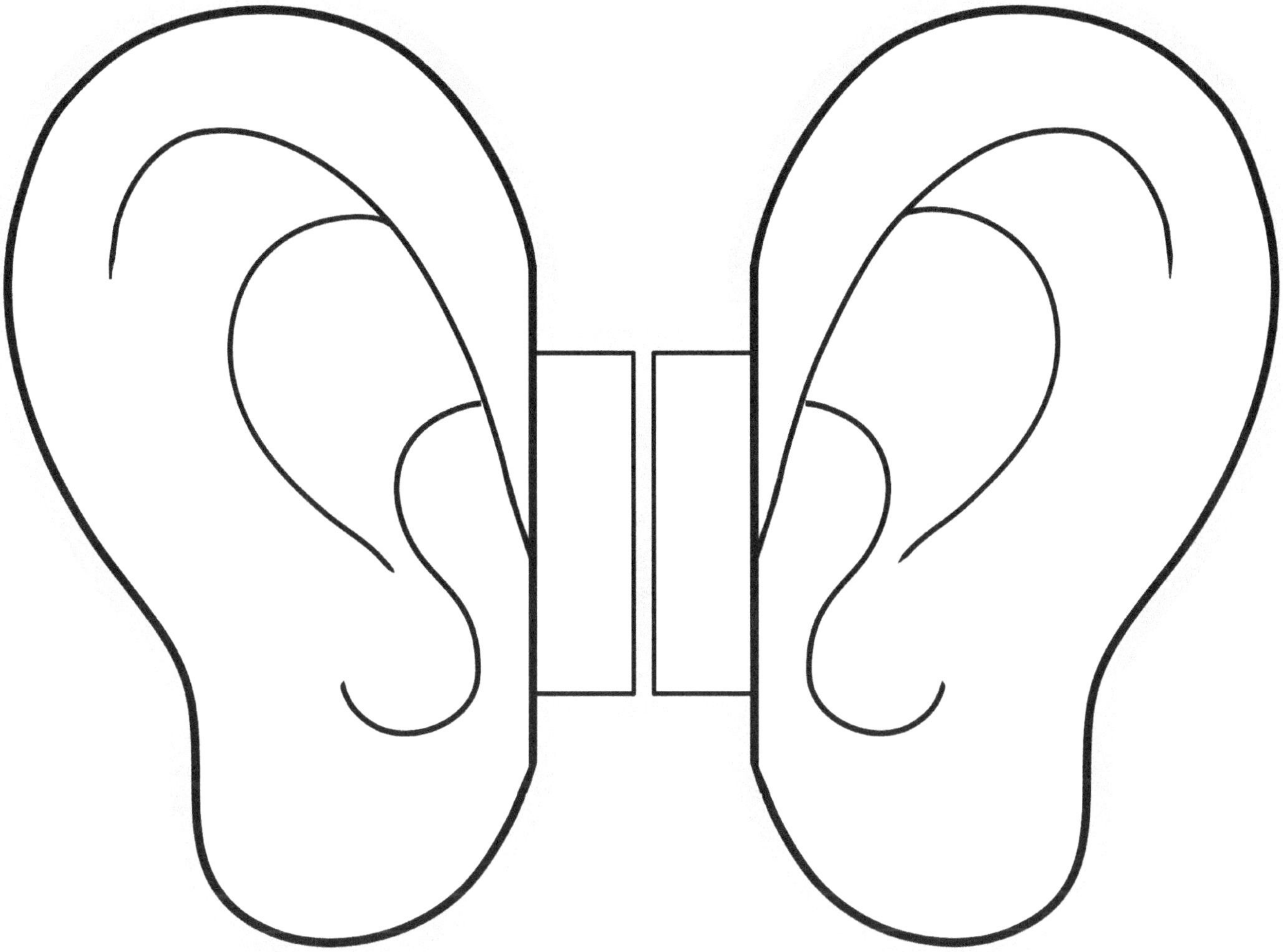

Story
20

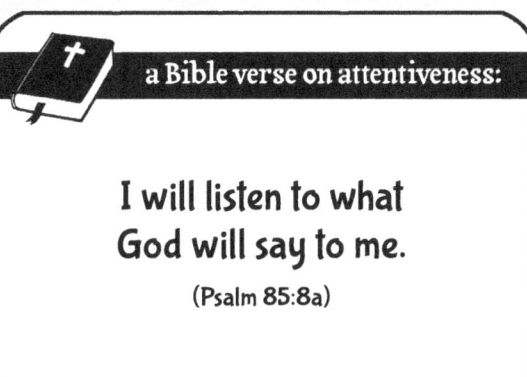

a Bible verse on attentiveness:

I will listen to what
God will say to me.

(Psalm 85:8a)

Story
21

Story
21

Story **21**

Story
21

Story **21**

The Lord is my shepherd.

He makes me lie down in green pastures.

He leads me beside the quiet waters.

He comforts my soul.

He guides me in the right path, in honor of His name.

Even though I walk through dark valleys...

... I will trust and not be afraid...

...Because the Lord is with me.

His shepherd's staff is a help to me.

Story **21**

a Bible verse on caring:

Whenever you are able, do good to people who need help.

(Proverbs 3:27)

The Lord prepares me a delicious feast.

He anoints my head with oil.

I overflow with His blessings.

God's goodness and mercy are for me...

...and will be with me all the days of my life.

I will dwell in the house of the Lord forever.

Story
21

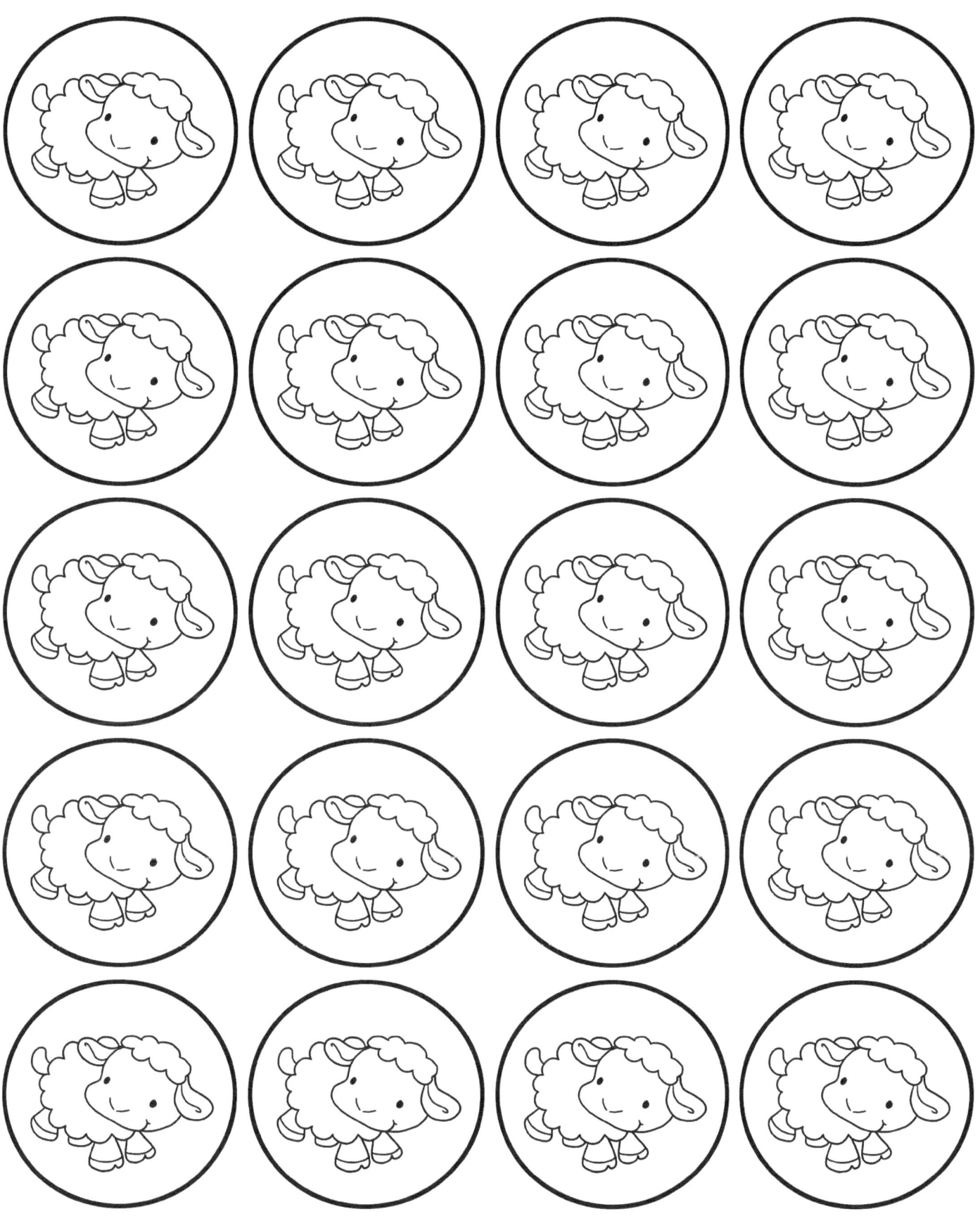

54

Write your name here:

The Lord is my shepherd. He gives me everything I need.

Make the shepherds clothes and staff out of color paper or cloth.
Let the dots help create them from simple shapes.

He lets me lie down in fields of green grass.

Cut and glue strips of green paper for the grass.
Glue some glitter on the moon and stars.

He leads me beside quiet waters.

Glue some blue colored paper or cloth over the water.
Add some cotton for the sheep's wooly coat.

He gives me new strength.

Add lots of heart shapes to show the shepherd's love for his sheep. Glue a bandaid on the sheep's leg, to help her feel better.

He guides me in the right paths for the honor of his name.

Trace over the words Jesus with a colorful marker. Cut out some rock shapes from grey paper and write on them some things that the Bible teaches us to do.

Even though I walk through the darkest valley,

Draw or glue around the page, some pictures of things that make you scared. Then finish the kids' faces to show how they might feel.

I will not be afraid because You are with me.

Use some colored paper to draw a set of hands. You can make the shape of your own hands if you like. Then glue them around the girl, to show God's hands keeping her safe.

You prepare a feast for me right in front of my enemies.

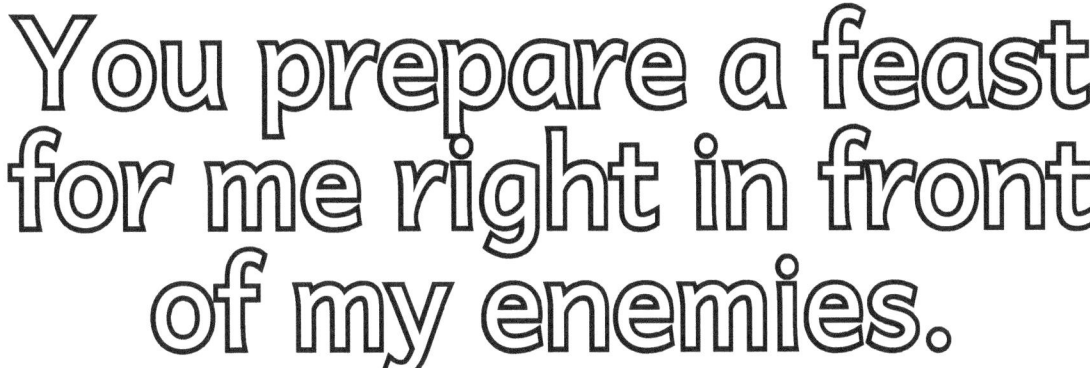

Draw or cut out from magazines, some pictures of your favorite foods and glue them on the plates and bowl. Then thank God for them!

You pour oil on my head and my cup runs overflows.

Cut out a picture of an oil bottle and glue it onto the bottle shape. Cut out some drop shapes out of yellow paper to make as the oil.

Your goodness and love will follow me all the days of my life.

Cut out some circle shapes for **GOODNESS** and some heart shapes for **MERCY**. Glue them onto the path, following the sheep, one after another.

And I will live in the house of the Lord forever.

Create God's House of out colored paper and shiny glitter, star stickers or sparkles and anything else you would like to add. Then color the full picture.

Story
22

Story **22**

U G

O A

C R E

✝ **a Bible verse on courage:**

Be strong and of good courage.
Don't be afraid; for the Lord
your God will go with you.

(Deuteronomy 31:6)

CLAP YOUR HANDS

JUMP UP FOR JOY

Story 23

KNEEL AND PRAY

72

LIFT HANDS AND PRAISE

Story
23

74

Story
23

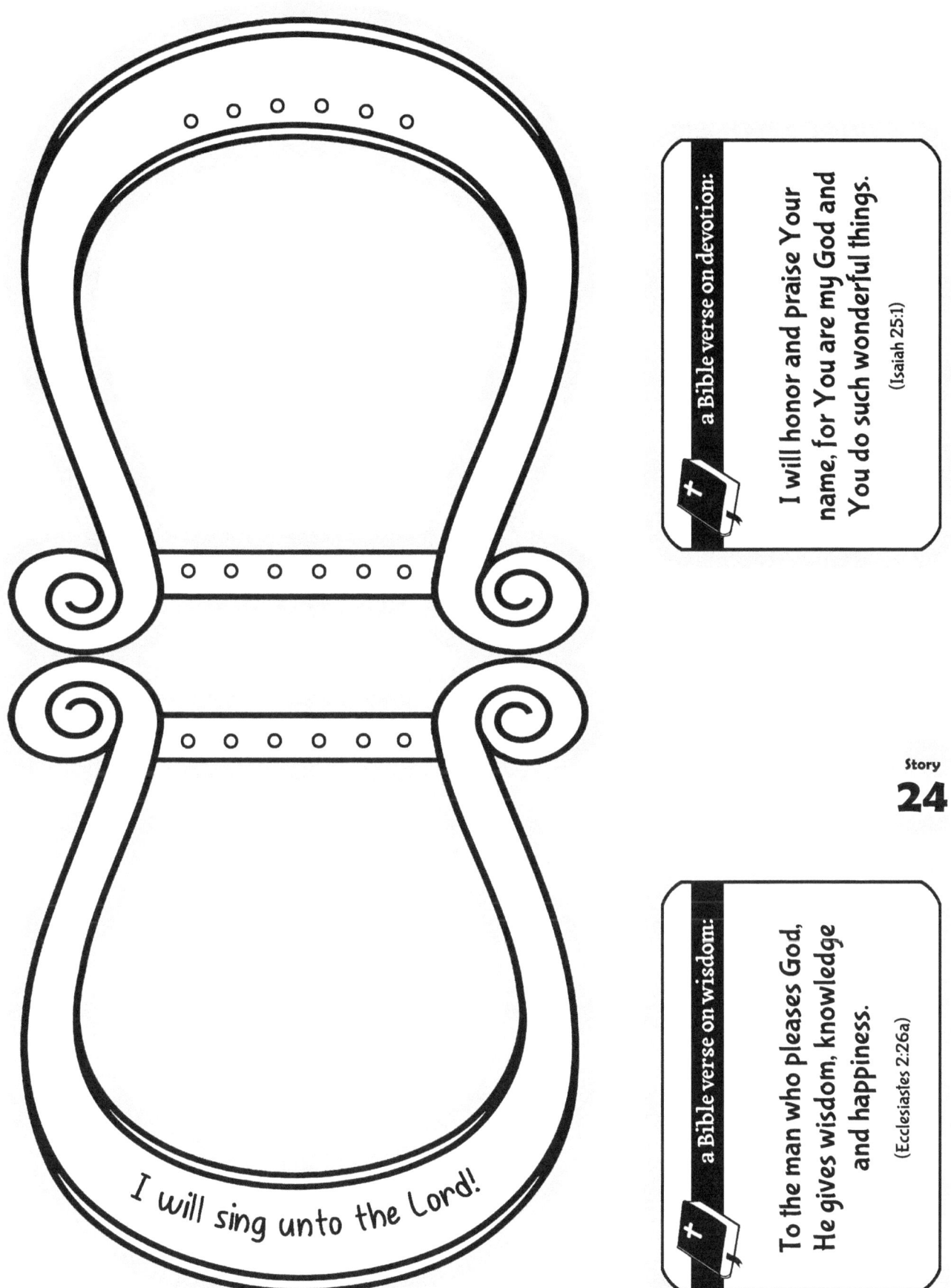

a Bible verse on devotion:

I will honor and praise Your name, for You are my God and You do such wonderful things.

(Isaiah 25:1)

Story
24

a Bible verse on wisdom:

To the man who pleases God, He gives wisdom, knowledge and happiness.

(Ecclesiastes 2:26a)

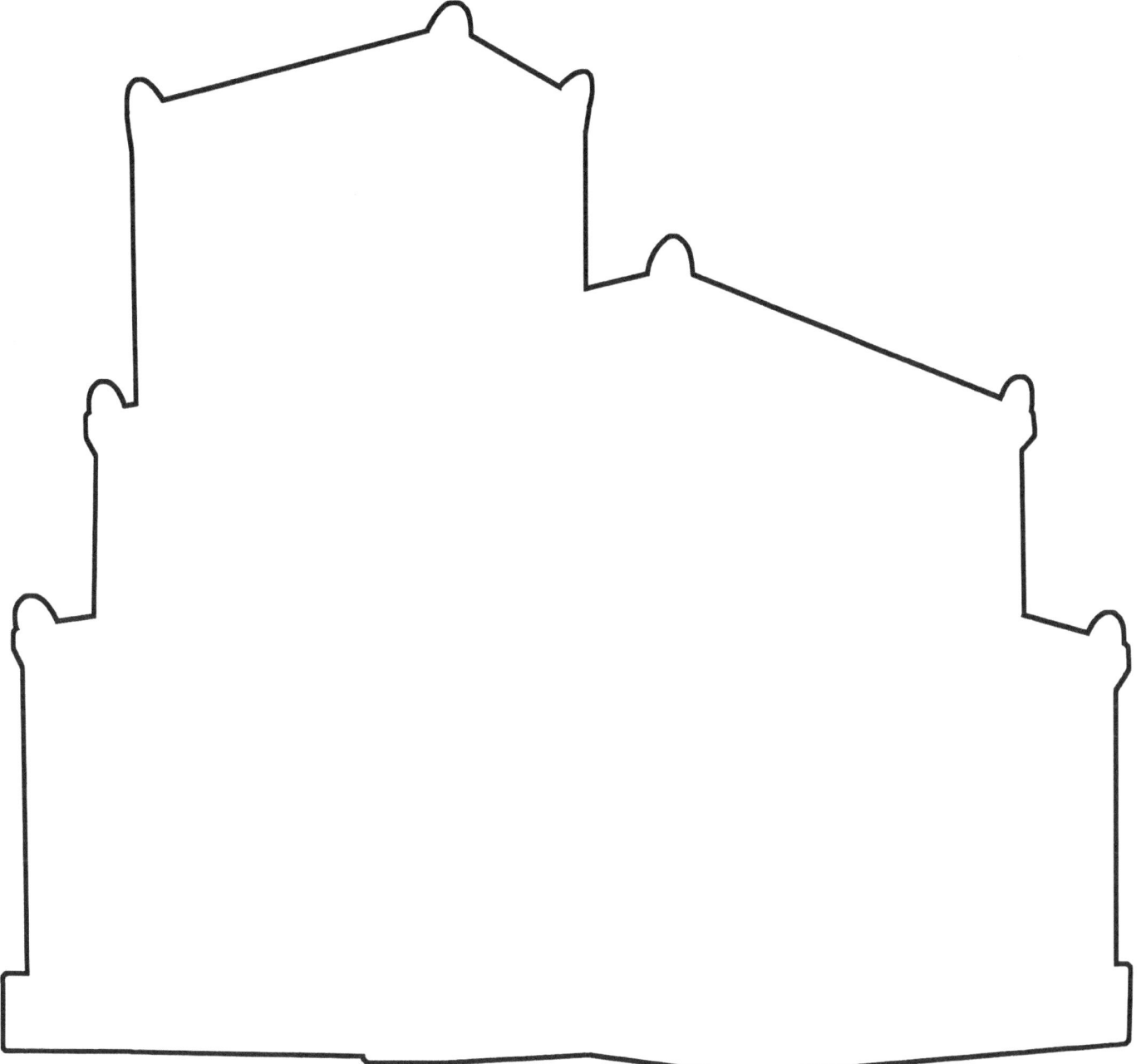

A temple for God

Story
25

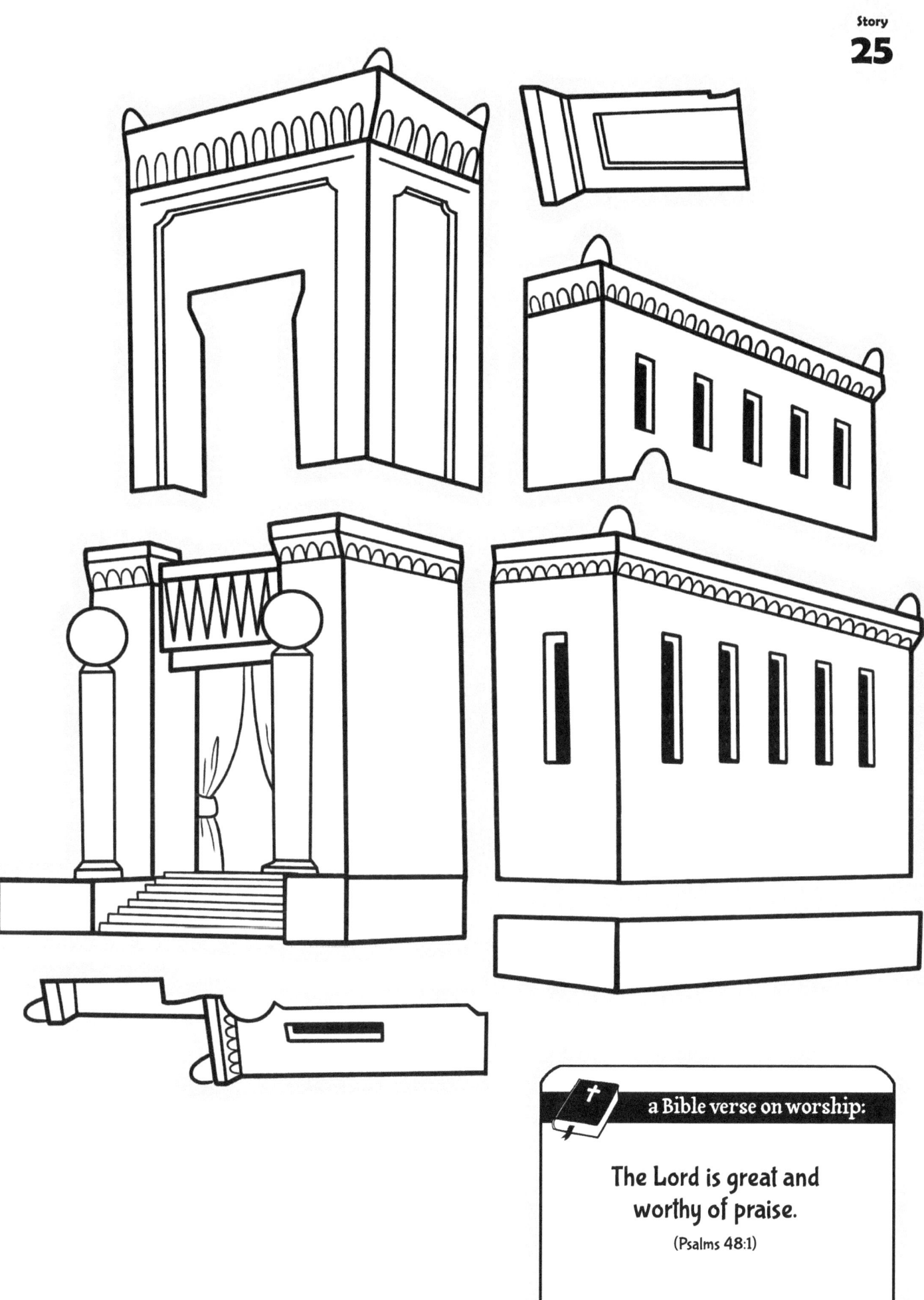

a Bible verse on worship:

The Lord is great and worthy of praise.

(Psalms 48:1)

Story
26

a Bible verse on endurance:

If you have endurance, you will finish what you've started and receive God's blessings.

(Hebrews 10:36)

Story
27

a Bible verse on unselfishness:

Don't just look out for yourself and think about your own good, but also think about the good of others.

(Philippians 2:4)

Story
26

Story
28

a Bible verse on determination:

Keep your eyes focused on what is right to do. Look straight ahead to what is good.

(Proverbs 4:25)

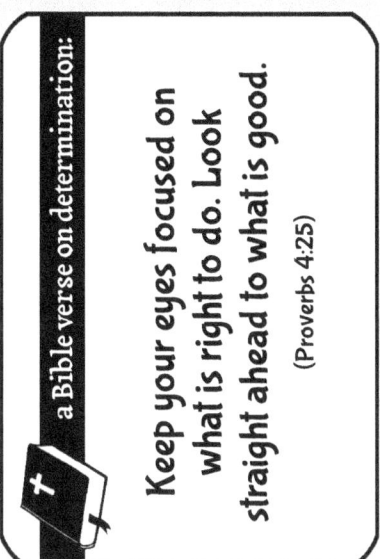

Keep your eyes focused on what is right to do.
(Proverbs 4:25)

Story
29

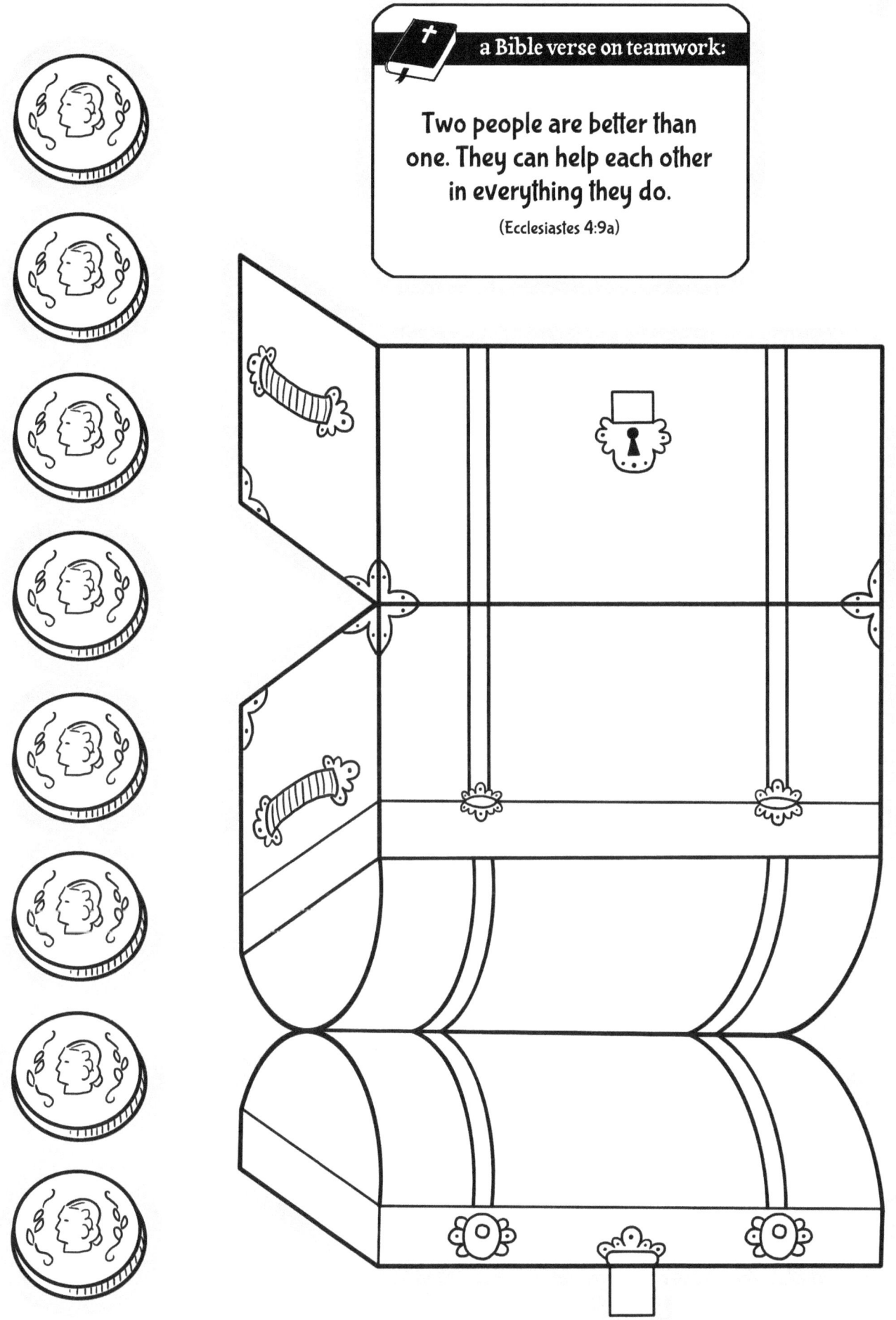

a Bible verse on teamwork:

Two people are better than one. They can help each other in everything they do.

(Ecclesiastes 4:9a)

Story 29

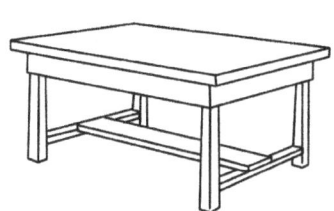
under

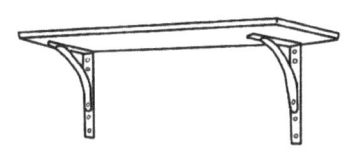
on top

beside

between

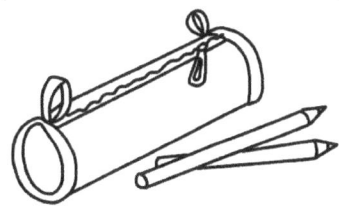
inside

near

behind

in front

close by

Story 29

under   **on**   **beside**

between   **inside**   **near**

behind   **in front**   **close by**

Story
29

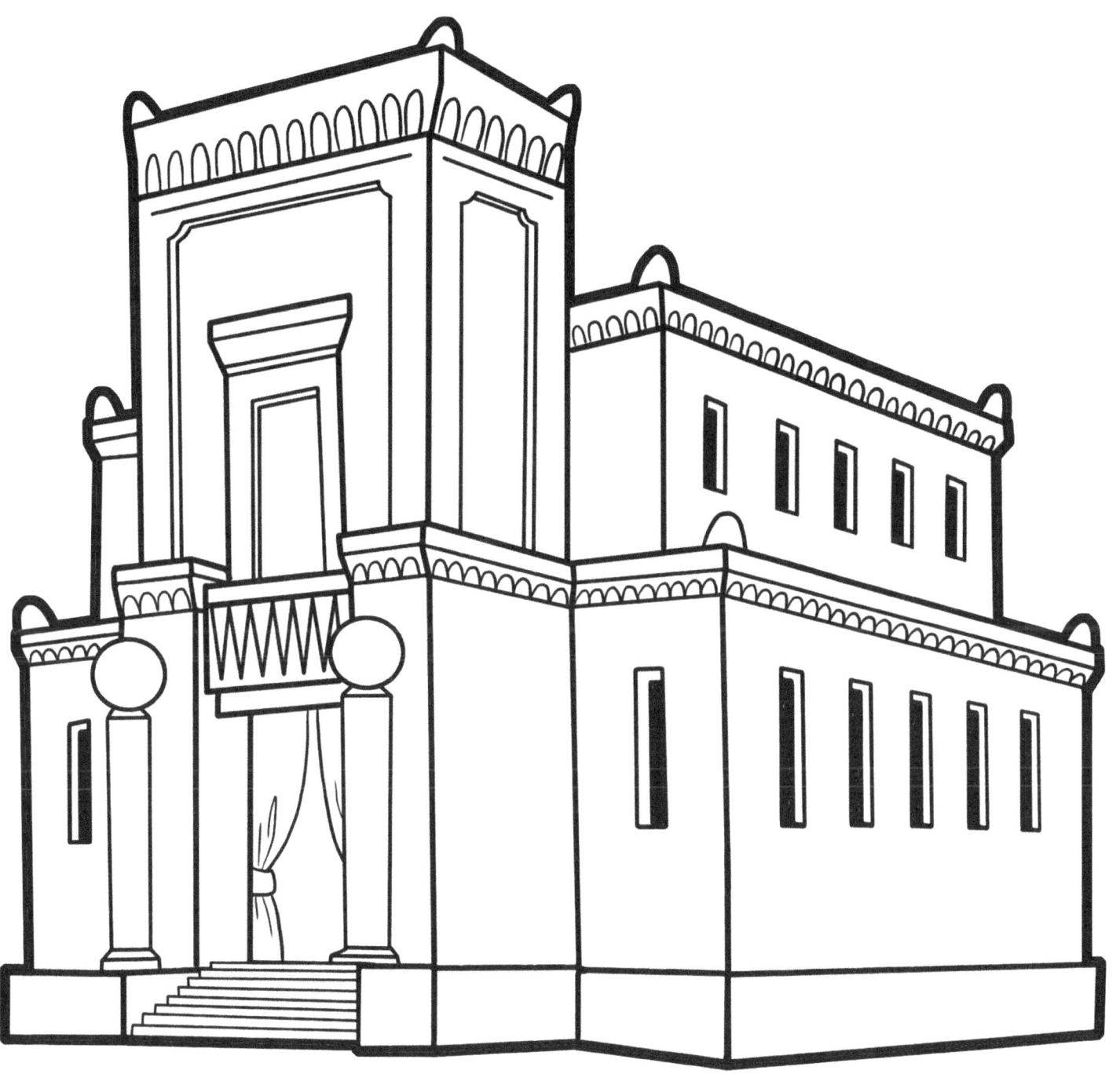

Story 29

Story
30

We have confidence and speak without fear. Philippians 1:14

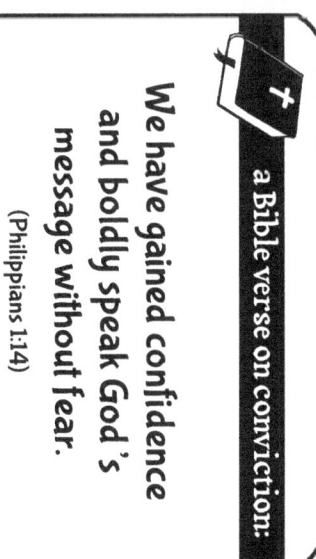

a Bible verse on conviction:

We have gained confidence and boldly speak God's message without fear.

(Philippians 1:14)

Story **32**

a Bible verse on perseverance:

Let us not be weary in doing things that are good.

(Galatians 6:9a)

Story **32**

Story **33**

a Bible verse on beauty:

True beauty comes from inside you. It is the beauty of a gentle and quiet spirit.

(1 Peter 3:3–4)

Story 34

a Bible verse on availability:

I desire to do Your will, dear God, because Your Words are in my heart.

(Psalm 40:8)

Story **35**

a Bible verse on God's love:

God loved us so much, that He sent us His only Son.

(John 3:16a)

Story **36**

a Bible verse on admiration:

I will honor You, my God and King. I will praise Your name forever and ever.

(Psalm 145:1)

Story
36

Story
37

 **a Bible verse on God's Word:**

The teaching of God's Word gives understanding.

(Psalm 119:130)

97

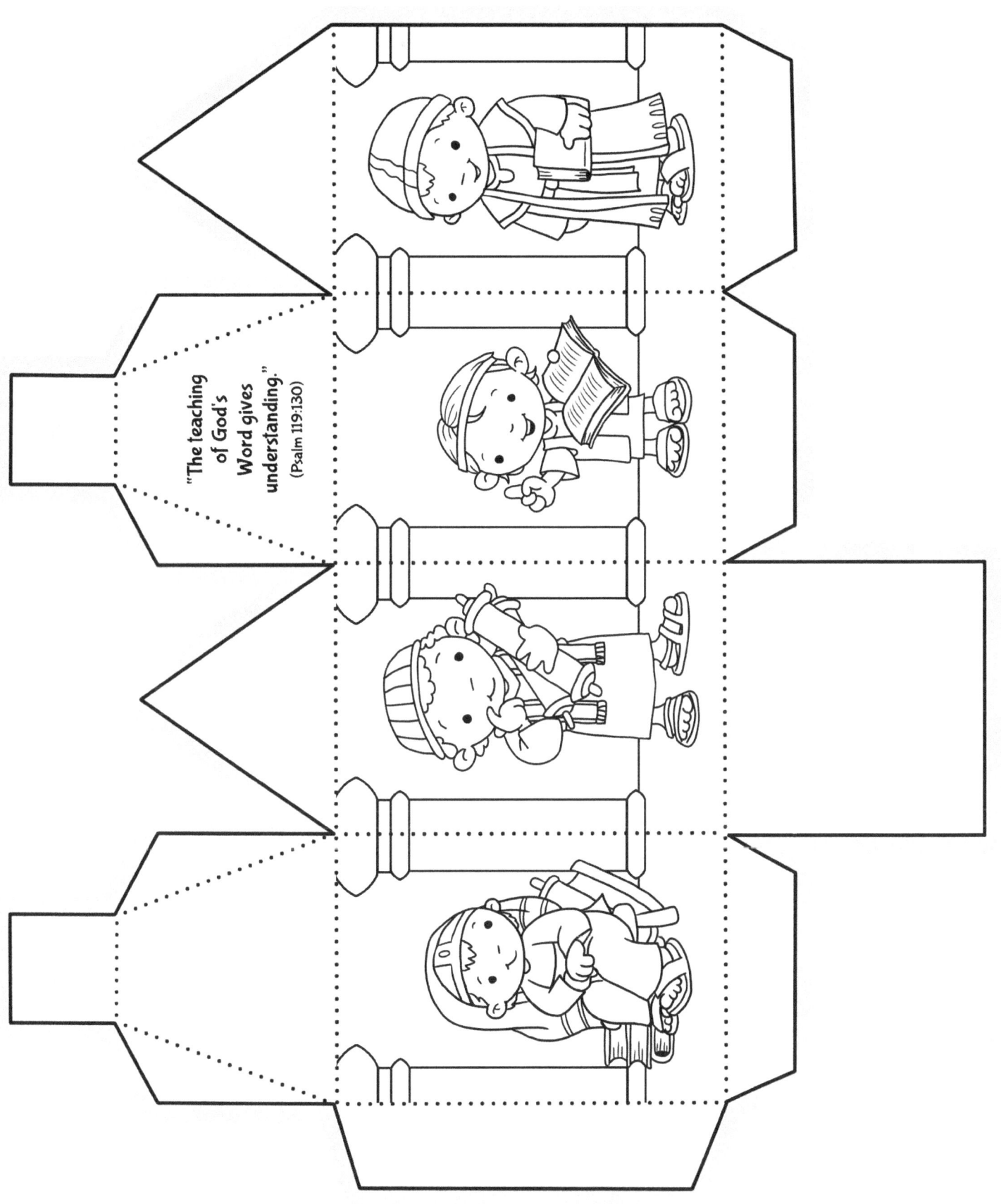

Story
38

99

Story
38

 a Bible verse on boldness:

May you speak the Word of God with all boldness.

(Acts 4:29)

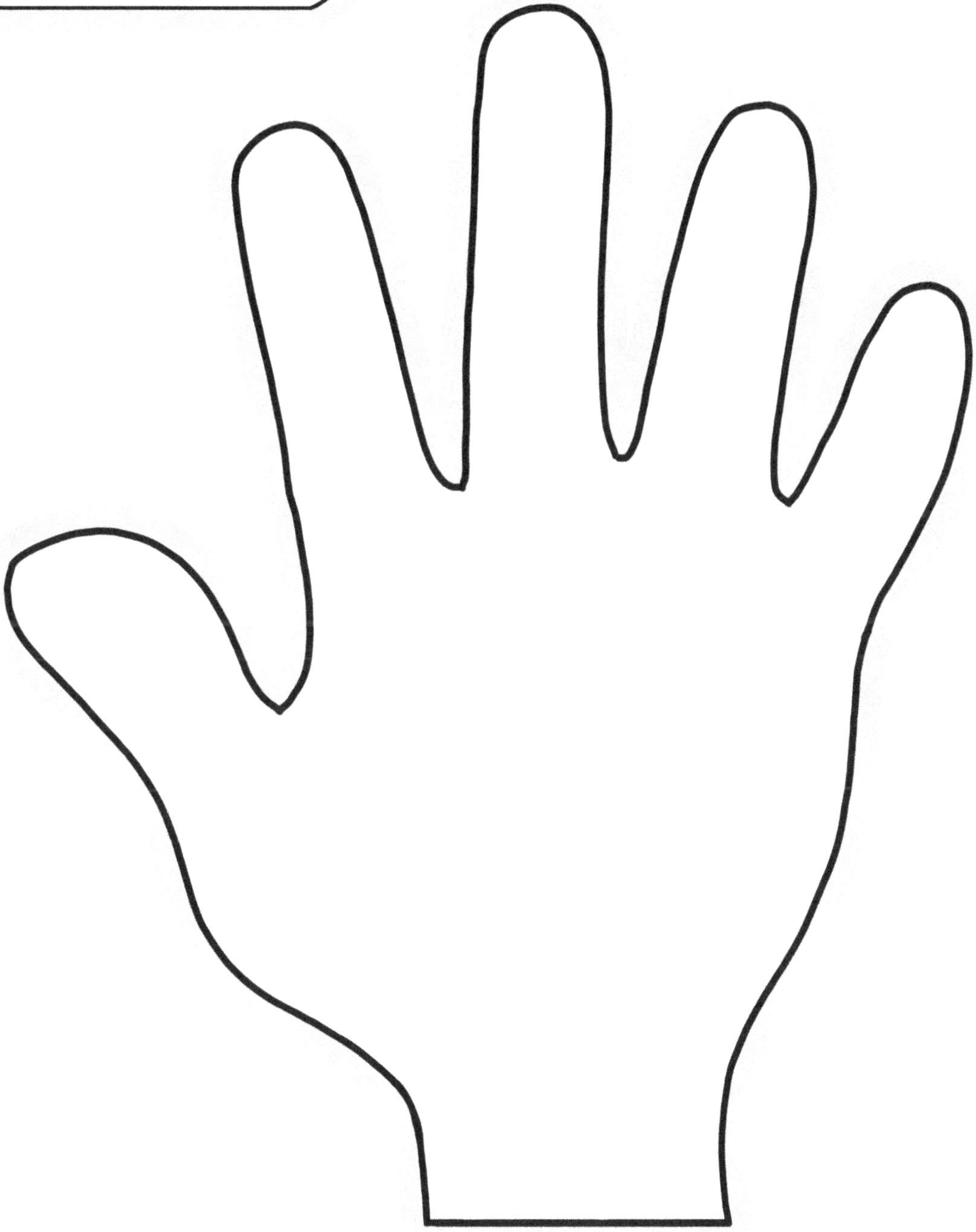

Story **39**

- Simon
- Thaddaeus
- Andrew
- Matthew
- Philip
- Thomas
- Peter
- Bartholomew
- John
- James
- Judas
- James

a Bible verse on following Jesus:

Jesus left us an example to follow and to do as He did.

(1 Peter 2:21b)

Story
39

102

Story
40

103

Story **40**

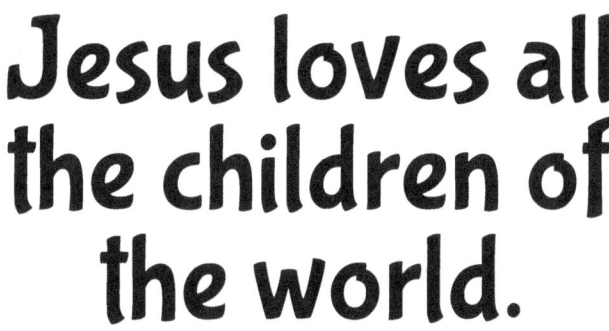

Jesus loves all the children of the world.

 a Bible verse on kindness:

Love is patient. Love is kind. Love never fails.

(1 Corinthians 13:4,8a)

Story **40**

Story
41

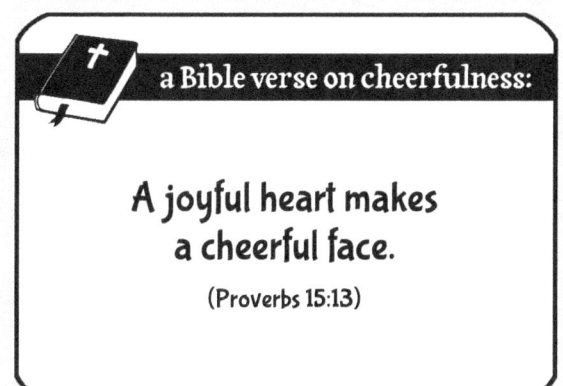

a Bible verse on cheerfulness:

A joyful heart makes
a cheerful face.

(Proverbs 15:13)

Story
41

Story 41

But we have no more wine.

We can't have our party without anything to drink.

What are we going to do? This is terrible!

Jesus will know what to do.

Let's do just what Jesus says to do.

Jesus will have a solution for us.

How can we fill the pots with just water?

The master of the party won't want water to drink?

If Jesus says to do it, I'll do it happily.

This is exciting. I wonder what Jesus will do.

Wow! Jesus did a miracle!

Now we have the best wine ever.

Story
42

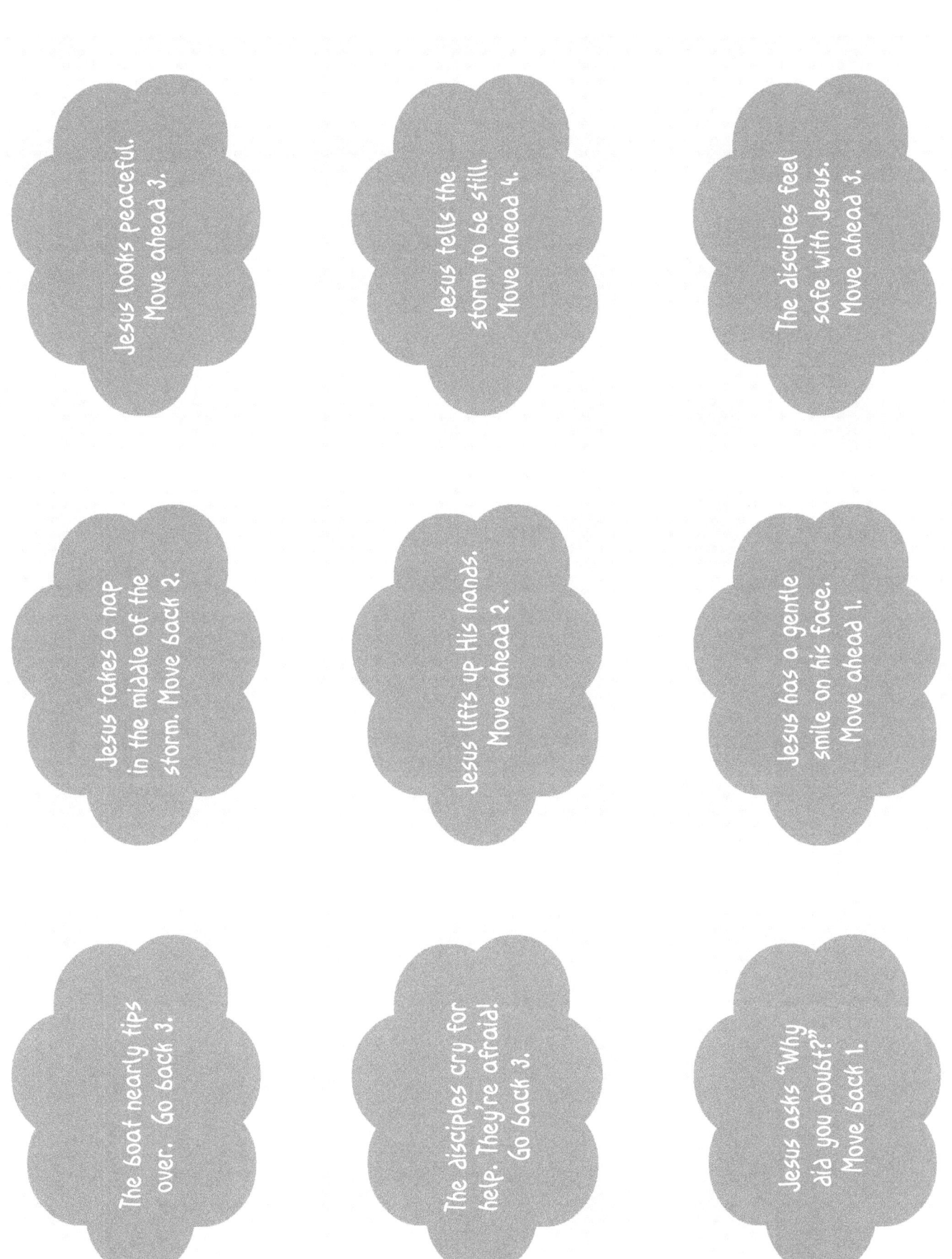

Story **42**

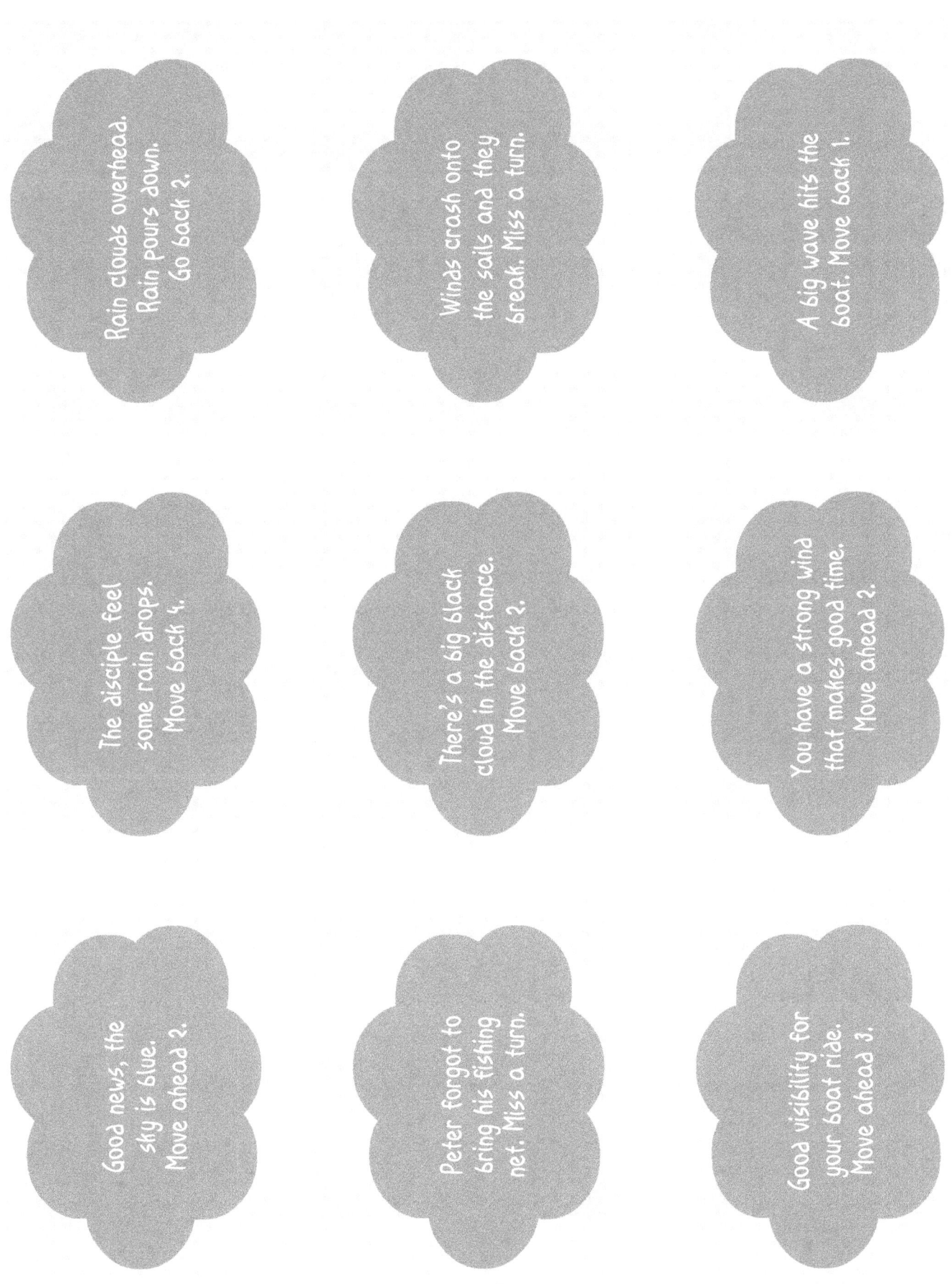

Story 42

- You can't find your missing shoe anywhere, and you'll be late for school.

- Your big brother or sister is too busy to spend time playing with you.

- Your friends are going on vacation, but you're not.

- It seems your brother or sister always get to pick what they want to do and you don't.

- It's been raining outside for days and you're bored at home.

- You don't have all the toys that you would like to have.

- You watched a scary movie at a friend's house.

- Your dad or mom has to go on a trip for work.

- You would like to play but you have to finish your homework first.

- Plans changed and you're not going to be able to go to your friend's house anymore.

- Your best friend is playing with other kids and not with you.

- You want to go to the fair, but your brother wants to go to the park.

Story
45

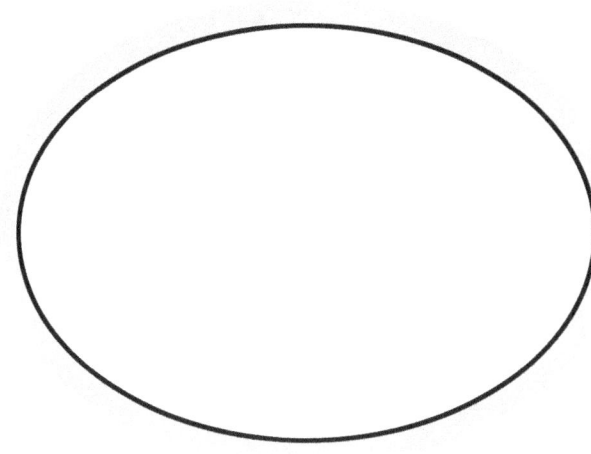

a Bible verse on responding:

Little children, let us not love in word or talk but in deed and in truth.

(1 John 3:18)

a Bible verse on faith:

A prayer full of faith will save those that are sick and God will make them better.

(James 5:15)

Story
43

a Bible verse on friendship:

A man that has friends must show himself friendly.

(Proverbs 18:24)

Story
46

Glue together here

Story **46**

A man that has friends must show himself friendly. A friend stays closer than a brother.

(Proverbs 18:24)

Glue here   Glue here

Glue here

Story
46

leaping

walking

praising

laying

Story
47

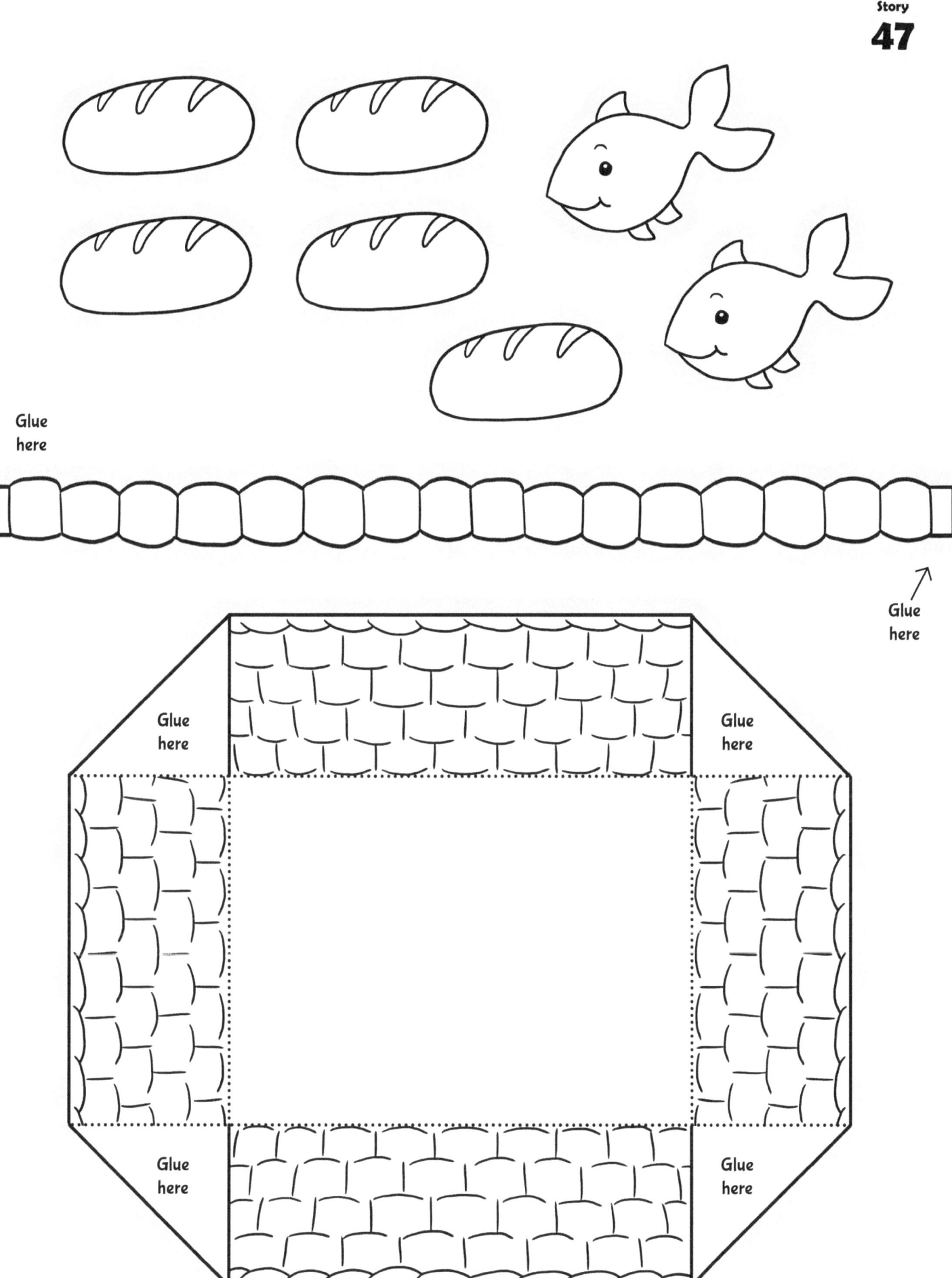

Story
47

a Bible verse on sharing:

Be generous and ready to share with others.

(1 Timothy 6:18)

Story
48

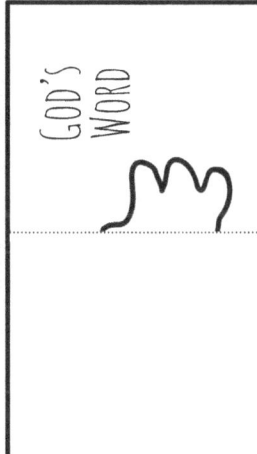

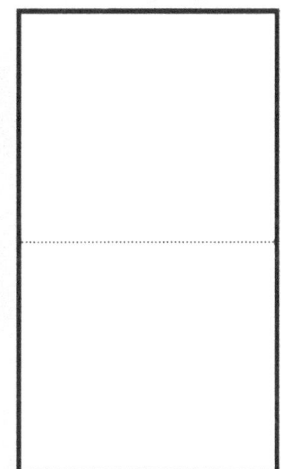

a Bible verse about time for Jesus:

Put God first, in everything you do, and He will guide your way.

(Proverbs 3:6a)

Story 49

 **a Bible verse on compassion:**

God is merciful and gracious, full of love and faithfulness.

(Psalm 86:15)

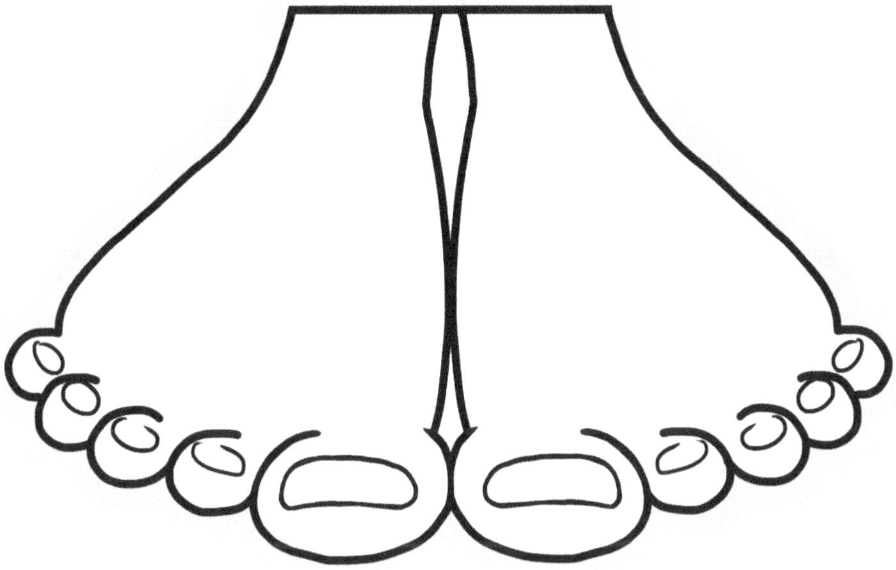

Story
49

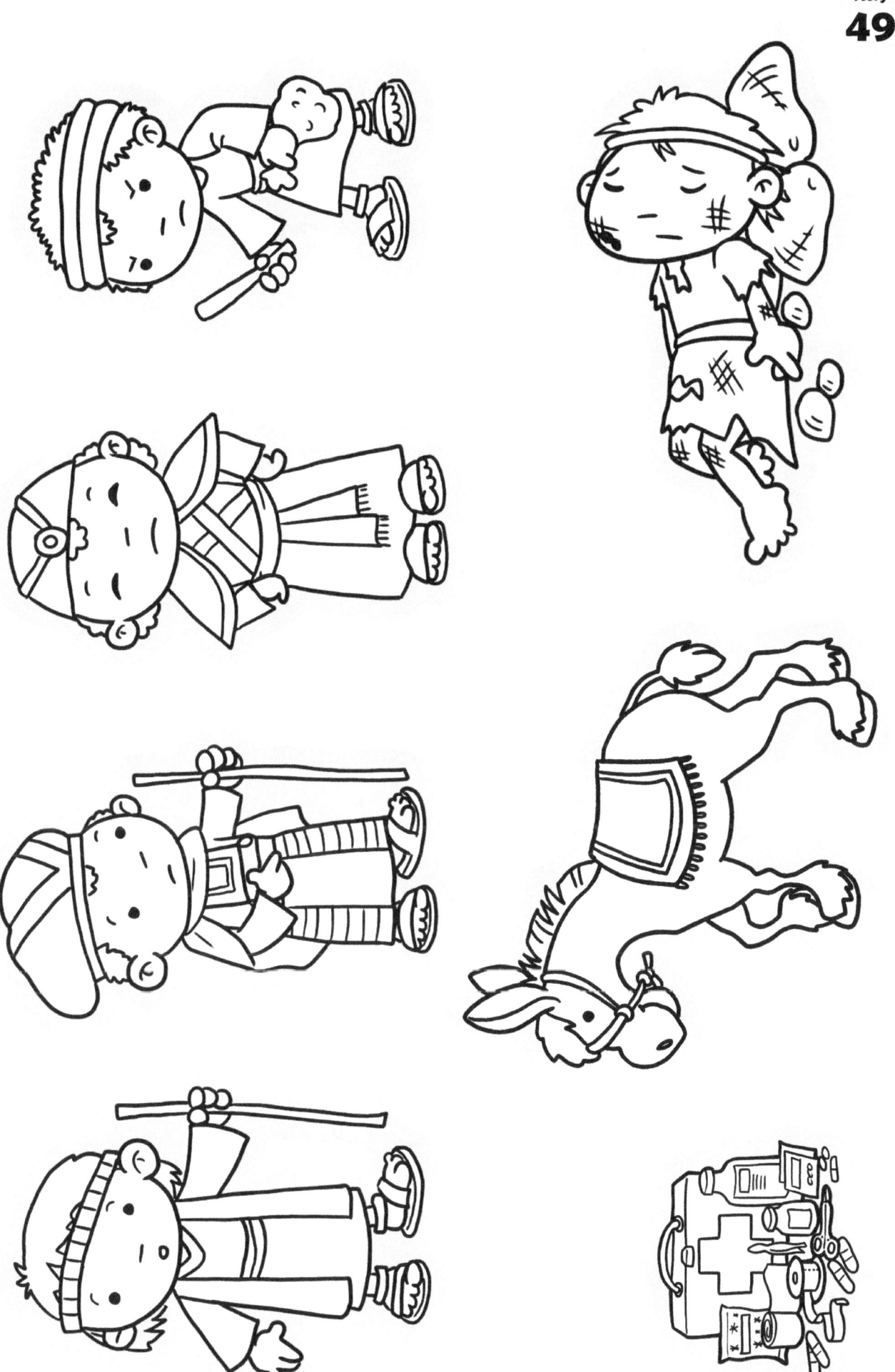

123

Story 50

a Bible verse forgiveness:

Where there are big sins, God's grace and goodness is even bigger.

(Romans 5:20)

Story
51

 a Bible verse on gratefulness:

Give thanks in all things,
for this is obeying and
pleasing to God.

(1 Thessalonians 5:18)

Story
52

 a Bible verse on repentance:

If we confess our sins,
He will forgive us and show
us a better way to live.

(1 John 1:9)

Story **52**

127

Story
53

a Bible verse on enthusiasm:

This is the day that the Lord has made. Let's rejoice and be glad about it.

(Psalm 118:24)

Story
54

 **a Bible verse on communion:**

Each time you eat this bread and drink this cup, remember Me.

(1 Corinthians 11:24–25)

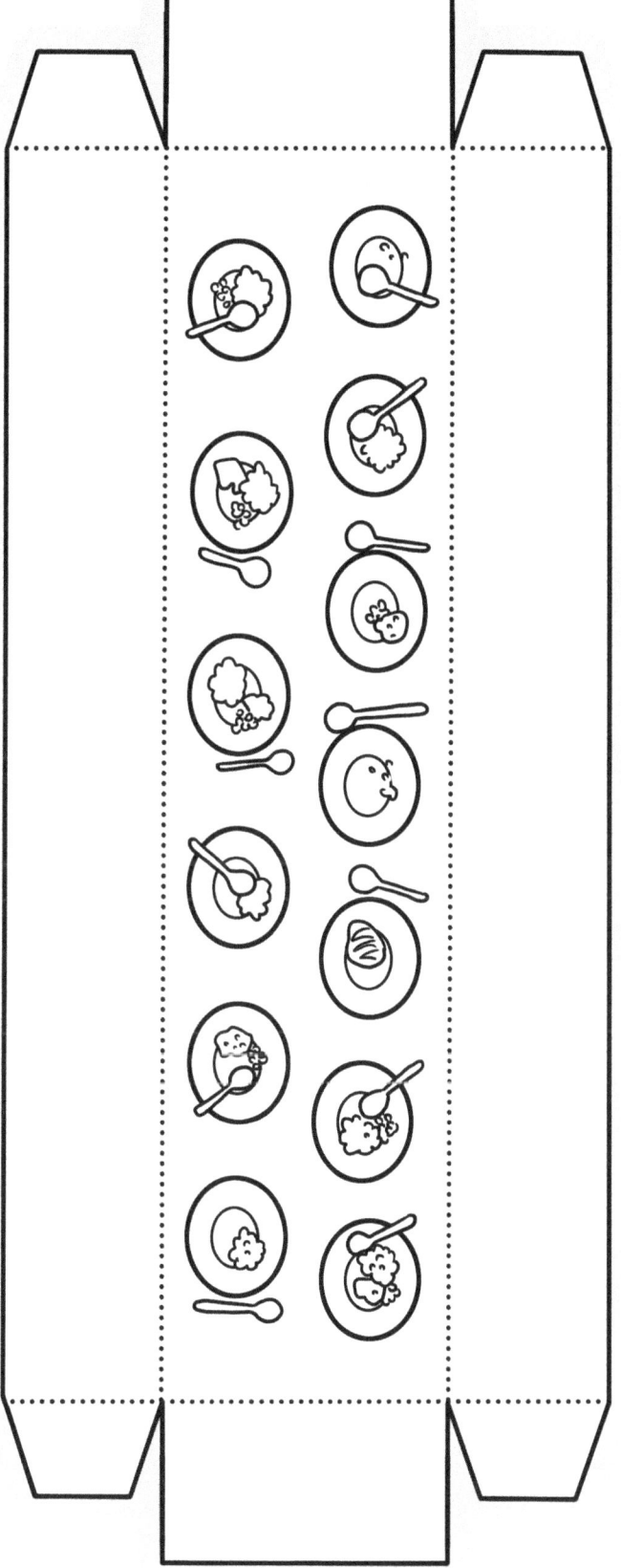

Story
54

130

Story
55

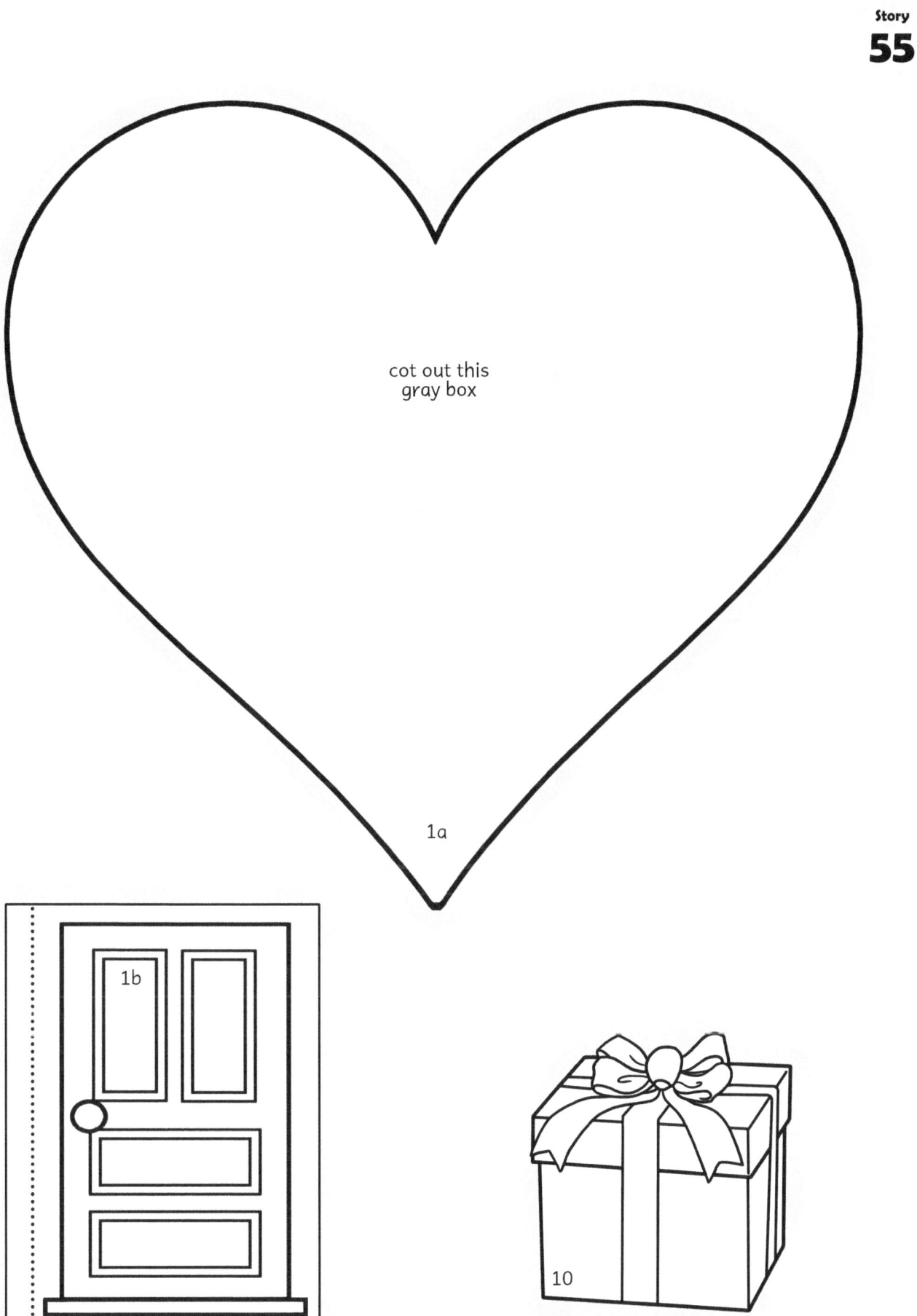

Story **55**

 a Bible verse on salvation:

Whoever believes in Jesus will never die, but will live with Him forever.

(John 3:16b)

Story
56

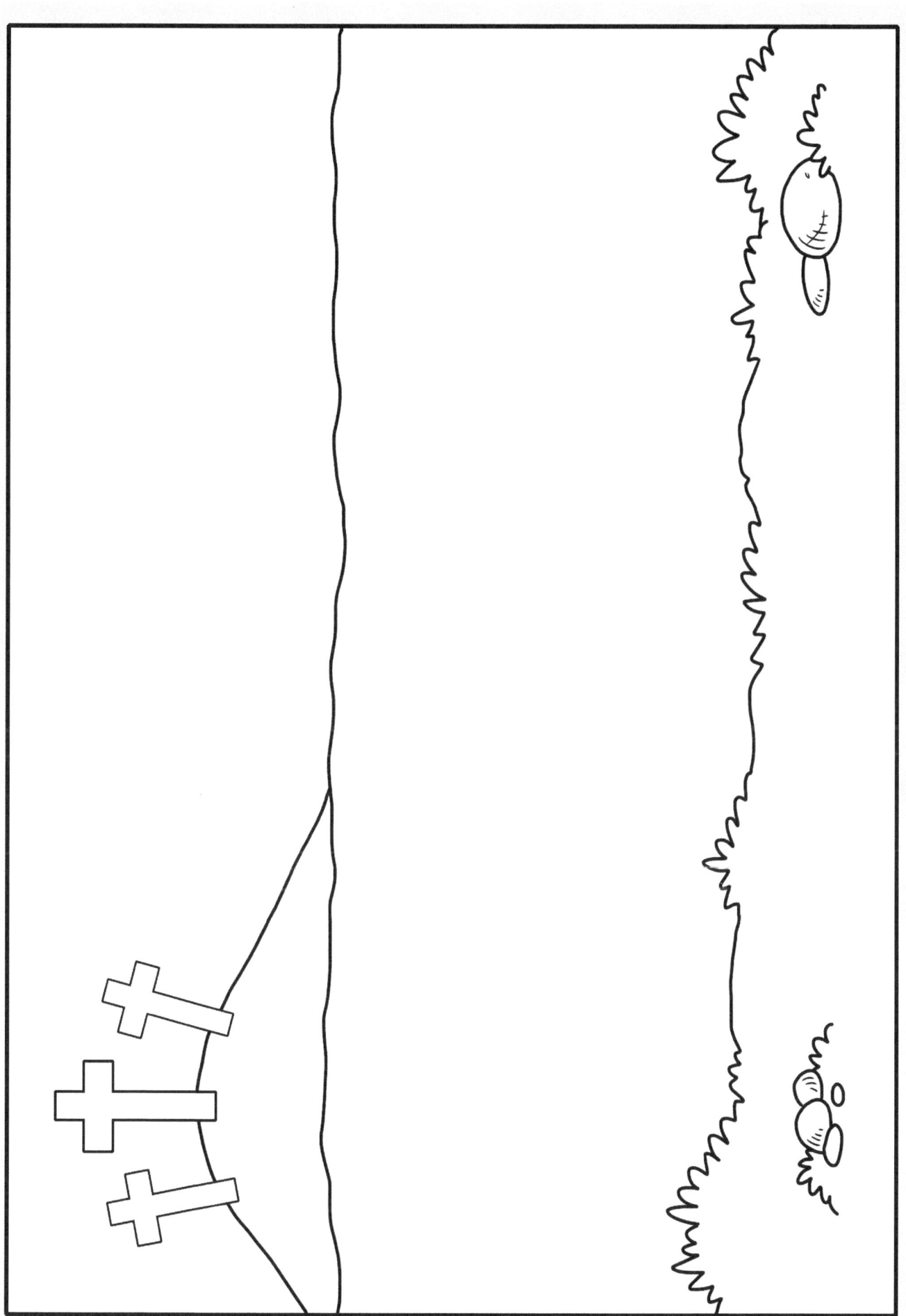

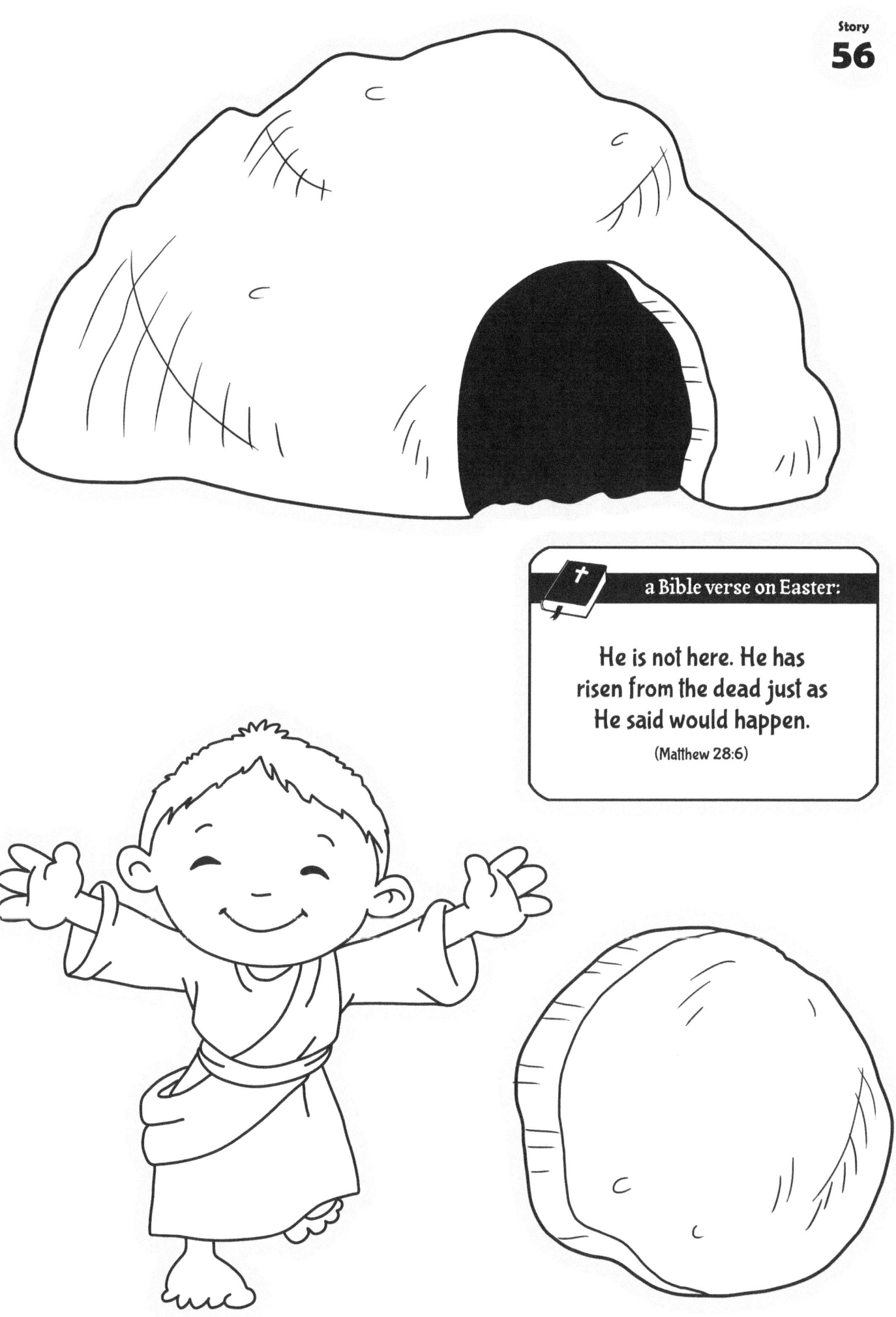

Story **56**

- Let's celebrate Easter!
- Jesus rose from the dead, as He said He would.
- Don't delay, share the good news right away!
- Hooray! Jesus is alive again!
- We love Jesus and He loves us.
- Jesus died to save us from our sins.
- We will live with Jesus forever in heaven.
- Jesus is real and He lives in our hearts.
- Jesus is the only One who rose from the dead.
- Do you believe in Jesus? Yes, I do.
- Jesus is God's son.
- Jesus is the resurrection and the life.

If you believe in Jesus, you will live forever.

Easter gives us a message of hope.

Rejoice and Praise; for He is raised.

Story
58

 love

 courage

share the good news

faithful witness

 boldness

 prayerful

 enthusiasm

praise

a Bible verse on the Holy Spirit:

The Holy Spirit will come to you and you will be My witnesses in every part of the world.

(Acts 1:8)

Story 58

truthful

thankful

joyful

happy

We are filled with **love** through the Holy Spirit. Romans 5:5	God fills us with **joy** through the Holy Spirit. Romans 15:13	The Holy Spirit helps us to tell the **truth**. John 16:13
The Holy Spirit helps **remind** us of things. John 14:26	The Holy Spirit gives us peace and **trust**. John 14:27	The Holy Spirit fills us with God's power so we can be **STRONG**. Ephesians 3:16
The Holy Spirit helps to **teach** us. John 14:26	Luke 12:11-13 The Holy Spirit gives us the **words** to say.	The Holy Spirit helps us to tell others about **Jesus**. Acts 1:8

Story 59

a Bible verse on witnessing:

Go and tell the good news of Jesus to the whole world.

(Mark 16:15)

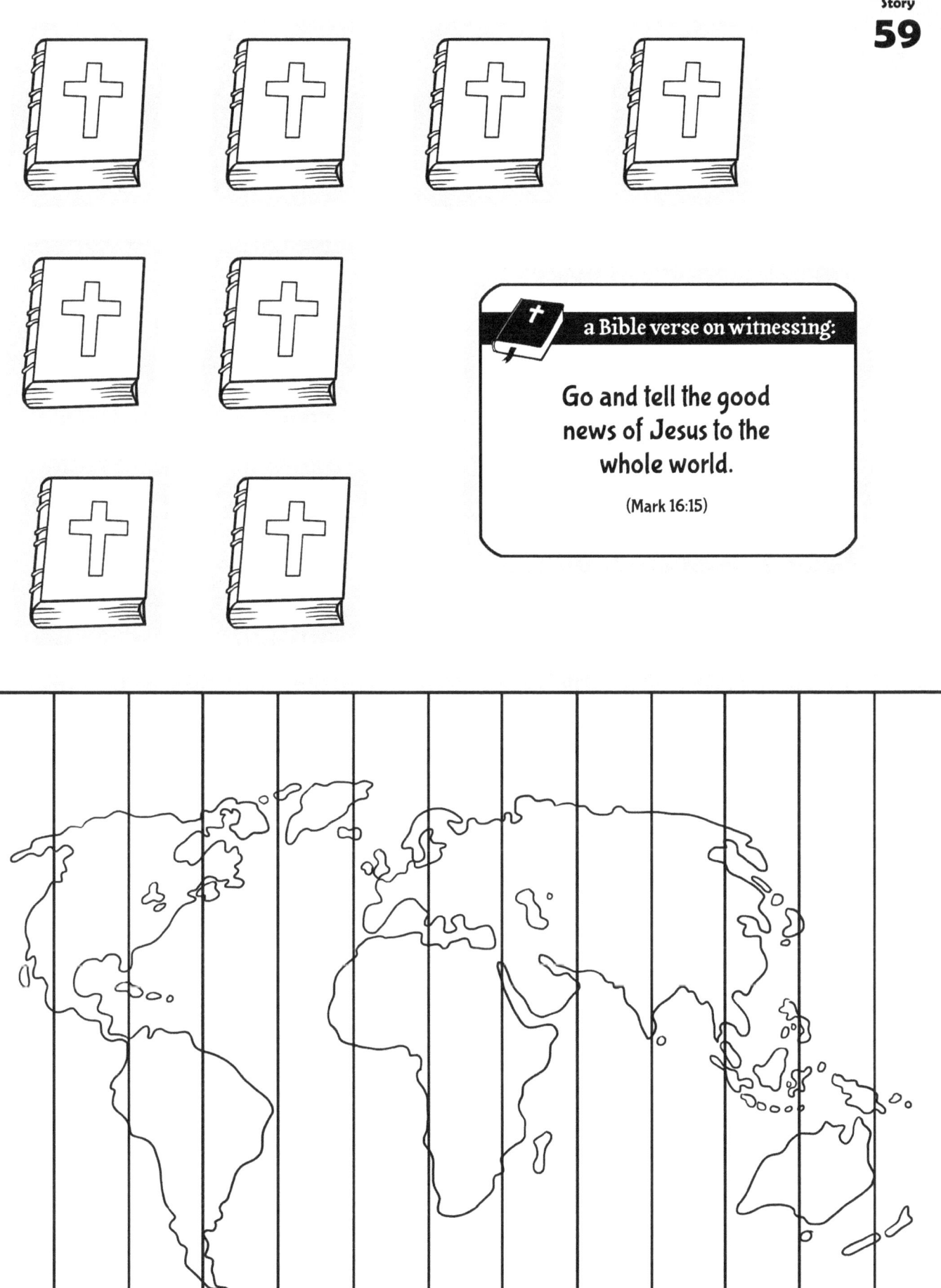

Story **59**

GOOD NEWS

GOD IS GOOD!

Jesus loves you!

God's love lasts forever.

Jesus died to forgive our sins.

Jesus saves!

He gives eternal life.

JESUS IS ALWAYS WITH ME!

Story
60

Story **60**

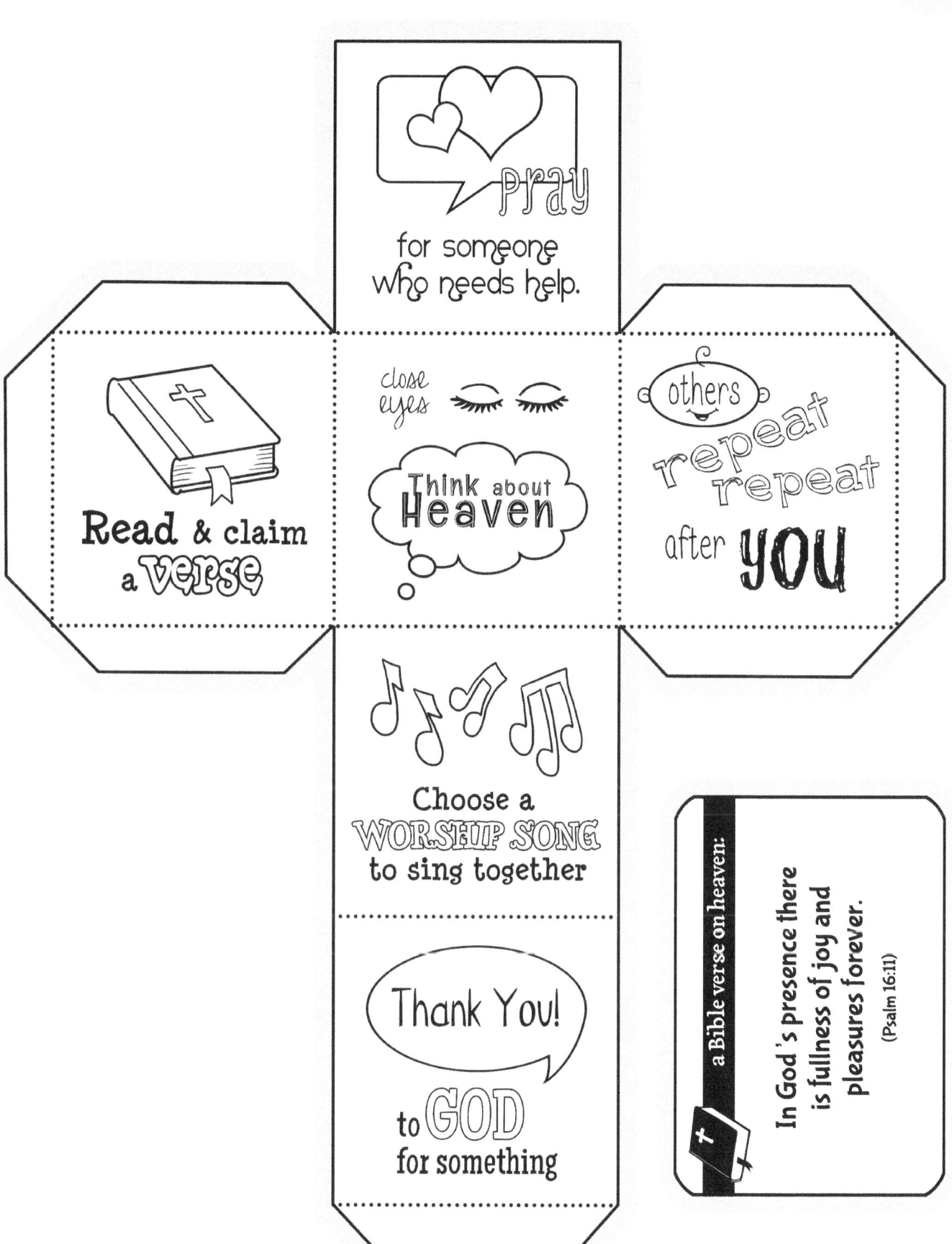

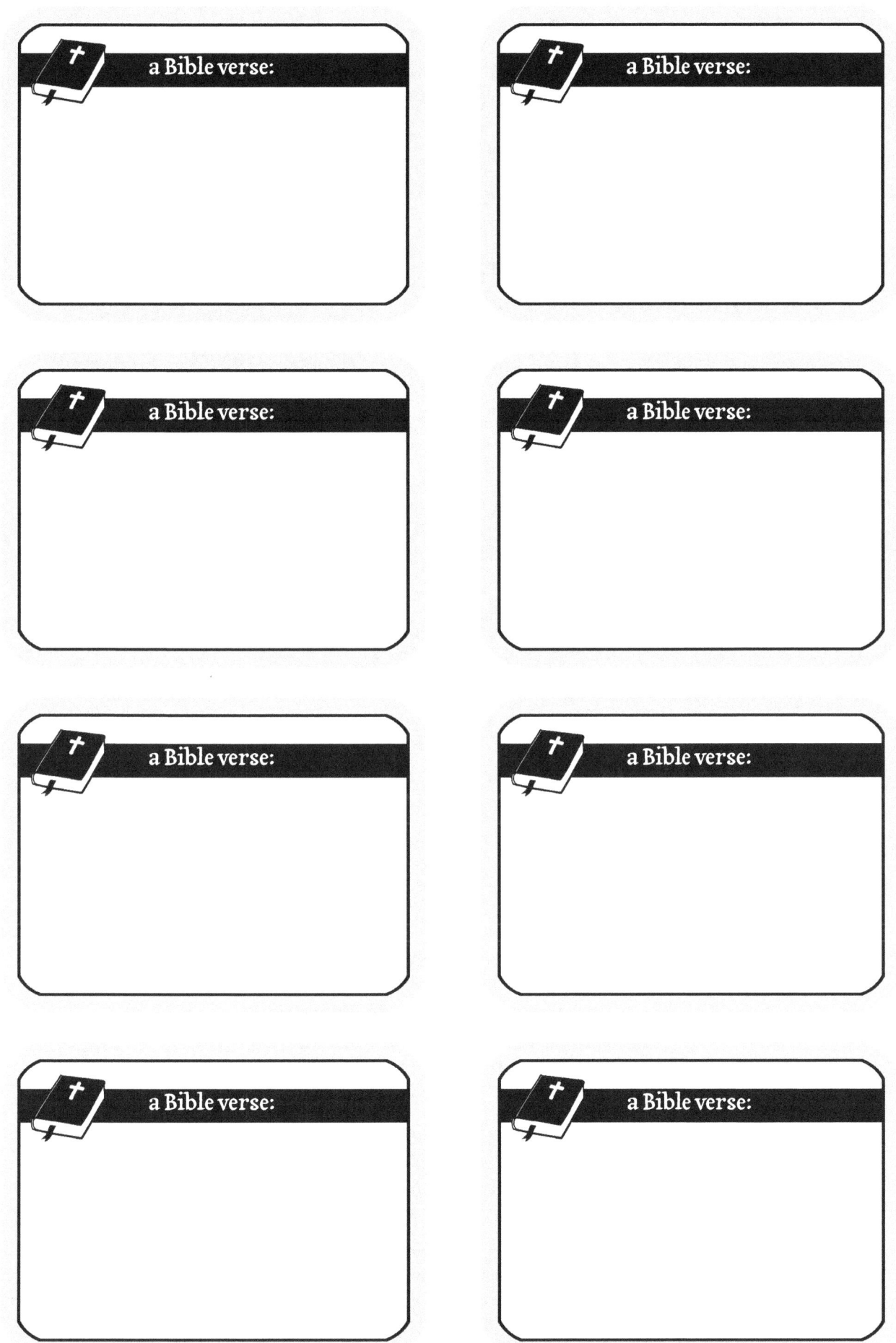

Don't miss getting your own copy of the book "Big Bible, Little Me". It features 60 charming Bible stories with colorful illustrations, verses and everyday story examples that will help children to apply lessons of value and character, all the while increasing their love and understanding of God's Word.

Published by iCharacter Ltd. (Ireland)
Created by Agnes de Bezenac
Illustrated by Agnes de Bezenac
All Bible verses adapted from the KJV.
Copyright. All rights reserved.
www.iCharacter.org

Follow us on Facebook: www.facebook.com/icharacter
See us on YouTube: www.youtube.com/icharactervideos
Follow us on Twitter: www.twitter.com/icharacternews

Copyright © 2016 iCharacter Ltd. All rights reserved. No part of this book may be reproduced in any form or by any electronic or mechanical means, including information storage and retrieval systems, without written permission from the publisher or author, except in the case of a reviewer, who may quote brief passages embodied in critical articles or in a review.
(Note: You may only photocopy one copy for each of your <u>immediate</u> students.)

www.ingramcontent.com/pod-product-compliance
Lightning Source LLC
Chambersburg PA
CBHW080026080526
44586CB00017B/2138